Resurrection

Resurrection

John Bunyan

Sovereign Grace Publishers, Inc.
P.O. Box 4998
Lafayette, IN 47903
http://www.SovGracePub.com

Printed In the United States of America
By Lightning Source, Inc.

PUBLISHER'S STATEMENT

A great many of the most powerful authors in the English language were puritans in 17th-century England. John Bunyan must be counted such a powerful writer.

Apart from language specialists, it can be said that few regard Elizabethan English as the ideal instrument to convey an idea in the 20th Century. So, in order for you to get the impact and the unspeakable beauty of Bunyan's God-guided missiles of love, we have taken the liberty of bringing this treatise up-to-date in language. In addition, sentences have been shortened, new subjects and verbs supplied, with some deletion of repetitive matter also-- it is our belief and prayer that Bunyan's intention and thought is preserved in all cases.

As a further help to the reader, we are using THE LIVING SCRIPTURES (a new translation in the King James tradition) in an attempt to have immediate understanding a certainty as you read the proof verses of God's Word.

Since virtually everyone must translate Elizabethan English as they read it (saying to themselves constantly, "this means that") no doubt you will be glad that the above-mentioned changes have been made.

Now may our God and Saviour, even Jesus the Creator and Judge of us all, lead you into all His truth revealed in this book.

JAY GREEN, Publisher

CONTENTS

Courteous Reader:

Though this is but a small book, yet it will present you with things of the greatest and most weighty concernment (the consideration of life and death to eternity.) It will open to you that the time is at hand when there shall be a resurrection of the dead, both of the just and the unjust—and this we will clear from the Scriptures of God. And this resurrection shall be a resurrection of the bodies of both the just and the unjust from the graves where they are, or shall be, at the approach of that day.

Also in these few lines, you have the order and the manner in which these two sorts of people shall rise; and you will be shown the kind of body which shall rise, as well as their state and condition at that day.

For here you shall see the truth and the manner of the terrible judgment, the opening of the books of God, the examining of witnesses, with a final conclusion upon good and bad. This, I hope will be profitable to your soul as you read it. For if you are godly, then here is that which will through God's blessing encourage you to go on in the faith of the truth of the Gospel. But if you are ungodly, then here you may meet conviction. Yes, you shall meet with that which will be your end at the end of the world, whether you continue in your sins, or repent. If you continue in your sins, you will meet with blackness and darkness and everlasting destruction. But if you repent and believe the Gospel, then you will meet with light and life and joy and comfort, with glory and happiness—and that to eternity.

Therefore, let me ask these things from you:

1. Be careful that you do not have that spirit of mockery that says, "Where is the promise of His coming." (1 Pet. 3:9)

2. Be careful that your heart shall not become burdened down with self-seeking, drunkenness and the cares of this life—lest that Day come upon you before you know it.

3. Be diligent to make your calling and election sure (2 Peter 1:10), so that you shall not be found without that glorious righteousness that will stand you in good stead and present you before His glorious presence with exceeding joy in that Day.

To Him be glory in the church by Christ Jesus, world without end. Amen.

JOHN BUNYAN

THE RESURRECTION OF THE DEAD
AN EXPOSITION OF ACTS 24:14,15

"But I confess this to you, that according to the Way(which they call heresy), so I serve the God of the fathers. I believe all things that have been written throughout the Law and the Prophets, having a hope in God which they themselves also hold, that there is going to be a resurrection of the dead, both of the just and the unjust."(24:14)

My discourse on this text will chiefly concern the resurrection of the dead. Therefore I will not meddle with anything else which may be in these words.

You see that Paul upon his arraignment was accused of many things, by those Jews who violently sought his blood. And when the Apostle was allowed to speak for himself by the heathen judge— he told them in a few words that he was utterly blameless as to those crimes which they had charged upon him. But this he confessed, that as to the Way, which they called heresy, so he worshipped the God of his fathers, believing all things that are written in the Law and the Prophets. And he had the same hope towards God which they themselves allowed, that there would be a resurrection of the dead, both of the just and the unjust.

From this, take note that a hypocritical people will persecute in others those truths which they themselves profess ("I have hope towards God, and that such a hope as they themselves allow, and yet I am today persecuted by them for this very thing").

But to come to my purpose, "There shall be a resurrection of the dead,"etc. By these words the apostle shows us what was the substance of his teaching, that there would be a resurrection of the dead. And by these words he shows what supported his soul through those temptations, afflictions, reproaches and necessities which he met with in this world— even this teaching of a resurrection: "I have hope towards God," he says, and thereby my mind is fixed, "for there shall be a resurrection of the dead, both of the just and unjust." The reason why I cannot do what these Jews would have me do, and the reason why I cannot live as the Gentiles live, is because I believe in the Resurrection with all my soul. This is the teaching which makes me fear to offend God, this is that which undergirds my soul, by which I am kept from destruction and confusion under all the storms and tempests I go through in this world. This is that which has more effect on my conscience than all the laws of men, despite all the penalties they inflict. "And in this I exercise myself to have a conscience without offense toward God and men continually" (Acts 24:16).

Now then, since this doctrine of the resurrection of the dead has the power both to bear us up and to awe us, both to encourage and to keep us within compass, the spirit and the body of the people of God, it will be necessary and profitable for us to inquire into the true meaning and nature of this word, "the resurrection of the dead."

WHAT IS MEANT BY THE DEAD?

The "dead" in Scripture go under a fivefold consideration:

1. The "dead" are those who die a natural death, as when a man ceases to be in this world. For example, Peter tells us that David "is both dead and buried," (Acts 2:29).

2. There is a people that are reckoned "dead in trespasses and sins," being those who have never been translated from darkness to light, from the power of Satan to God. These have never felt the power of the Word and Spirit of God, to raise them from that state, to walk with Him in the regeneration, making a life out of Christ and His present benefits.

3. There is a death which seizes upon men after some measure of light received from God, after some profession of the Gospel of Christ. These, because of the certainty of their condemnation, are said to be dead, dead: "twice dead, plucked up by the roots" (Jude 12).

4. There is in Scripture mention made of a death to sin and the lust of the flesh. This death is the beginning of true life and happiness. It is a certain forerunner of a share in Christ, of life with Him in another world.

5. Lastly, there is also in the word a relation of eternal death. This is the death that those are in when they go out of this world Godless, without Christ and without grace. These are dying in sin, and so they are under the curse of the dreadful God. These, because they have missed the Lord Jesus Christ, the Saviour in this day of grace, have fallen into the jaws of eternal death and misery, into "the fire that shall never be put out." (Mark 9).

WHAT IS MEANT BY THE RESURRECTION?

Since there is a "death," a being "dead" in so many ways in the Scripture, it is evident that our text is not meant of all of them. Then we must distinguish and inquire from which of these deaths that the apostle looked for a resurrection.

1. First then, it cannot be meant of a resurrection from eternal death—for from eternal death there is no redemption.

2. Secondly, it is not a resurrection from that double death (twice dead), for they that are in that death are also past recovery.

3. Thirdly, it is nonsense to say there shall be, or can be, a resurrection from death to sin, for that in itself is a resurrection from the dead. The apostle had passed through this resurrection, as he says, "He made us alive together with Christ" "who were once dead in trespasses and sins" (Eph. 2:1,4). Again, "If you then are risen with Christ;" and, "in which you were also raised with Him through the faith of the almighty working of God, who raised Him from the dead" (Colossians 2:12).

4. Lastly, by "the dead" then must be understood those who have departed from this life, those that have body and soul separated from each other—therefore the resurrection must be that of the body out of the grave. Daniel said, "Many that sleep in the dust of the earth shall awake, some to everlasting life, and some to shame and everlasting contempt" (Dan. 12:2). And the Lord said, "The hour is coming in which all those in the graves shall hear His voice and shall come forth..." (John 5:28,29).

The resurrection of the just, then, is the rising of the bodies of the just. And the resurrection of the unjust is the rising of the bodies of the unjust, at the last Judgment. This also is the meaning of Paul's words to Agrippa, "I stand, being judged for the hope of the promise made to the fathers by our God," (Acts 26:6). This promise at first began to be fulfilled in the resurrection of the body of Christ and has its accomplishment finally when the dead are raised out of their graves.

Christ has already risen, and thus far the promise is fulfilled. But His saints are yet in their graves, and therefore that part of the fulfilling is yet to come, as he says, "Why is it thought unbelievable by any of you that God raises the dead?" (Acts 26:8).

Again, that it is the resurrection of the dead bodies of both saints and sinners which Paul mentions is further evident because he says that it is the very resurrection that the Pharisees themselves hoped to attain, "now I stand, being judged for the hope of the promise made to the fathers by our God, the hope to which our twelve tribes hope to attain, serving God fervently night and day. It is concerning this hope that I am accused by the Jews," (vs. 7). Now we know that the Pharisees didn't believe in a resurrection from a state of nature to a state of grace, which is the same as the new birth. But they taught that they were the children of Abraham. Yes and when any of them in fact inclined to Christ's doctrine in some things, it was this doctrine of the new birth which they would most emphatically reject. Still, they were utterly against the teaching of the Sadducees, who denied the resurrection of the body.

Further, the resurrection spoken of here must be the resurrection of the body because it is called a "resurrection of the dead, both of the unjust and the just." That is, it was the resurrection of both saints and sinners—as Christ said, "The hour is coming in which all that are in the graves shall hear His voice and shall come forth—those who practiced good to the resurrection of life—and those who practiced evil to the resurrection of judgment" (John 5:28,29).

Lastly, the resurrection mentioned here is a resurrection of the future, one not already enjoyed by either saints or sinners, "there shall be a resurrection of the dead." Now I say that the resurrection which is here being desired by the just, which is that resurrection of the dead, both of the just and the unjust, is the same resurrection spoken of by Job, "so man lies down and does not rise. Till the heavens are no more, they shall not awake nor be awakened..." (Job 14:12).

EVIDENCE OF THE RESURRECTION OF THE DEAD

Now that I have opened this scripture to you, I shall now lay down for you several undeniable scripture demonstrations of the resurrection of the dead, both of the just and unjust. I do this for the satisfaction of those who are yet wavering, and for the refreshment of those who are strong and stedfast.

THE RESURRECTION OF THE JUST

1. The just must rise because "Christ has risen from the dead". Christ is the Head of the just, and they are the members of His body. Because of this union, then, the just must rise. This is Paul's own argument, "If Christ is preached, that He has been raised from among the dead, how do some among you say that there is not a resurrection of the dead. But if there is not a resurrection of the dead, neither has Christ been raised" (1 Cor. 15:12,13). The reason that the apostle argues the resurrection of the dead by the resurrection of Christ is this, that the saints (of whose resurrection he is here chiefly discussing) are in their bodies as well as in their souls the members of Christ. "Do you not know that you bodies are the members of Christ" –a very weighty argument, for if a good man is a member of Christ then he must either be raised out of his grave or else sin and death must have power over a member of Christ. If this body is not raised, then also Christ is not a complete conqueror over His enemies, for in that case death and the grave would still have power over His members. But "the last enemy put down is death"(see vs. 26). Even though Christ has a complete conquest over death in His own person, still death has power over the bodies of all those that are in their graves. Now if Christ is considered in His relation to His members, then He does not yet have a complete conquest over death, nor will He until every one of them has been brought forth out of their graves. For then, and only then, will that saying be in every way fulfilled, "Death was swallowed up in victory" (1 Cor. 15:54).

2. Secondly, there must be a resurrection of the just because the body of the saints, as well as their souls, has been purchased by Christ's blood, "You are bought with a price, therefore glorify God in your body and in your spirit, which are God's" (1 Cor. 6:20). And Christ will not lose that which has been purchased by His blood... Though the power of the grave is invincible, and though death is the king of terrors, yet Christ has the keys of hell and of death at his belt, for to Him belong the issues from death.

3. There must be a resurrection of the bodies of the righteous because our bodies are the temple of the Holy Spirit, "Or do you not know that your body is the temple of the Holy Spirit in you?" (1 Cor. 6:19). "But the body is not for

fornication, but for the Lord. And the Lord is for the body. And God has both raised up the Lord and will raise us up by His Power"(1Cor.6). The Lord is for the body, and not only in this world. He has raised up the body of Christ and He will raise up ours by Christ.

4. The bodies of the righteous must rise again because there is a necessary likeness between the body of the Lord Jesus and the bodies of the saints,"When He shall appear," then "we shall be like Him" (1 John 3:2). Now it is abundantly clear in Scripture that the body of the Lord Jesus was raised out of the grave and caught up into Heaven, and that it ever remains in the Holiest of all, a glorified body.

It would be very strange if Christ should be raised, ascended, glorified in that body and yet that His people would only be with Him only in their spirits. Since He is said in His resurrection to be but the first-begotten from the dead, and the first-fruits of those who sleep. Now a first-begotten implies more sons, and first-fruits foreshow an after-crop. We conclude, then, that "as all die in Adam, so also all shall be made alive in Christ. But each in his own order: — Christ the first-fruit; then they who are of Christ in His coming." (1 Cor. 15:22,23).

And so it is that the Scripture says, "who will completely transform our body (in which we are now humbled), for it to be made like His glorious body — according to the almighty working of His power, even to put all things under Himself"(Phil. 4:21). Again it is written that the day of Christ is to be the day of the unveiling of the sons of God (Rom. 8:19), and we groan as we wait for the adoption, "that is, the redemption of our body" (Romans 8:23). For then the saints of God shall not only be, but shall appear as their Saviour, being delivered from their graves, as He is from His. And they shall be glorified in their bodies, as He is in His.

5. There must be a resurrection of the body of the saints because the body as well as the mind has been a deep sharer in the afflictions that we have suffered for the sake of the gospel. Yes, the body is oftentimes a greater sufferer in all the   calamities that we undergo here for Christ's sake... It is in the body that we have the dying marks of the Lord Jesus, "that the life of JESUS might be shown forth in our body too. "

God is so just a God, so merciful to His people, that though the bodies of His saints should be ever so dishonorably tortured, killed and sown in the grave through the malice of the enemy, yet He will raise them again in incorruption, glory and honor. As He says in another place, that we who have continued with Christ in His temptations, that have undergone the rreroach and malice of the world for His sake, "and I appoint a kingdom to you, as My Father has appointed to Me" (Luke 22:29); "If we suffer with Him, we shall also reign with Him" (Romans 8:17); "And he who hates his life in this world shall keep it unto life eternal" (John 12:25). All this is to be enjoyed, especially at the resurrection of the just.

6. There must be a resurrection of the just, otherwise there will be the greatest disappointment on all sides that ever was.

The first disappointment is of the will of God: "And this is the will of the Father who sent Me, that of all which He has given Me I should lose nothing, but should raise it up again at the last day" (John 6:39).

There would also be a disappointment of the pwoer of God: For He who has raised up the Lord Jesus also intends to raise us up by His power, even our bodies. "Now the body is not for fornication, but for the Lord; and the Lord is for the body. And God has both raised up the Lord and also will raise us up by His own power" (1 Cor. 6:13,14).

Christ also would be disappointed of the fruits of all His sufferings to the point of wonderment. His people are the price of His blood, and the members of His body. And He is now at the right hand of God, far above all principalities and powers...expecting until His enemies are made His footstool, until they are brought under the foot of the weakest saint (Which shall not be until the last enemy, death, is destroyed. We know that He would come again and bring all His people to Himself, even up into Heaven, so that we might be where He is. But if when He comes, the grave and death has come before Him and hindered Him, keeping down those whom He had ransomed with His blood, would He not be disappointed?

If the bodies of the just do not arise from the dead, then the just also will be disappointed. It is true that the departed saints have far more fellowship and communion with God and the blessed Lord Jesus than we have, or are yet capable of having; but for all that, though they are there, they very much long for the day in which they will and must arise from the dead. This is the time that they long for when they cry under the altar, "How long, O Lord, holy and true, do You not judge and avenge our blood on those that live on the earth" (Rev. 6:10). When they died they died in hope to obtain a better resurrection. And now that they are gone, they long until the day is come—when the dead, even all the enemies of Christ shall be judged. For then He will give reward to His servants the prophets, and to the saints, and to those who fear His name, small and great (Rev. 11:18).

If the just do not arise, there will be great disappointment for the saints who are yet alive in this world. For although they have received the first-fruits of the Spirit, they wait not only for more of that, but also for the resurrection, redemption and changing of this vile body. "For our citizenship is in Heaven, from which also we are looking for the Saviour, the Lord Jesus Christ, who shall change our body of humiliation so that it may be fashioned like His glorious body, according to the working by which He is able even to subdue all things to Himself" (Philippians 3:20,21). But if the body does not arise, then how can it be made like the glorious body of Christ Jesus? Yes, what sad disappointment and delusion will it be to the poor creatures who look for such a thing, and that warranted by Scripture. They look for good, but behold, evil. They expect to be delivered in their whole man from every enemy, but lo! both death and the grave, their great enemies, swallow them up forever! But beloved, do not be deceived. The needy shall not always be forgotten. The expectation of the poor shall not perish forever. For Christ said, "everyone who sees the Son and believes on Him may have everlasting life. And I will raise him up at the last day" (John 6:40).

If the just do not arise out of their graves, then also every grace in our souls is defeated. For though the spirit of devotion can put forth a pretended show of holiness along with the denial of the resurrection, yet every grace of God in the elect prompts them forward to live as becomes the Gospel, by pointing to that Day.

FAITH looks at this, as it is written, "we also believed and therefore speak, knowing that He who raised up the Lord Jesus shall also raise us up by Jesus, and shall present us with you" (2 Corinthians 4:14).

HOPE looks at this, "we ourselves groan within ourselves, waiting for the adoption, the redemption of our body" (Rom. 8:23). That is, we expect this by hope. "But hope that is seen is not hope, for what a man sees, why does he still hope for it?" (verse 24).

SELF-DENIAL also works by this doctrine: "If according to the manner of men I have fought with beasts at Ephesus, what advantage is it to me if the dead do not rise?" (1 Cor. 15:32). As if he should say, Why do I deny myself of those mercies and privileges that the men of this world enjoy? Why do I not also shun persecution for the cross of Christ? If the dead do not rise, what shall I be the better for all my trouble that I meet with here for the gospel of Christ?

ZEAL and PATIENCE, with all the other graces of the Spirit of God in our hearts, are much, yes even chiefly encouraged, animated and supported by this teaching. "Be patient until the coming of the Lord..the farmer waits for the precious fruit of the earth and has long patience for it until he receives the early and the latter rain. You also be patient, establish your hearts, for the coming of the Lord draws near" (James 5:7,8)—when the dead shall be raised!

8. The doctrine of the resurrection of the just must certainly be the truth of God if we consider the devilish and fanatical errors and absurdities that must unavoidably follow the denial of it:

FIRST, he who holds that there is no resurrection of the body also denies the resurrection of the body of Christ. This is the Holy Spirit's own teaching, "But if there is no resurrection of the dead, then Christ has not risen" (1 Cor. 15:13). He who denies the resurrection of the members also denies the resurrection of the Head. For since the resurrection of the saints is proven by the resurrection of Christ, he who denies the first must also deny the second.

Now as this error is in itself destructive to all Christian religion, so it carries within its bowels many others as devilish:

(1) He who denies the resurrection of the saints concludes that it is vain to preach a deliverance from sin and death. For how can he be freed from sin who is swallowed up forever by death and the grave? Paul says, "And if Christ has not risen, then our preaching is vain and your faith is also vain" (verse 14).

(2) This error casts the lie in the face of God and of Christ and

of the Scriptures. "Yes, and we are found to be false witnesses of God, because we have testified of God that He raised up Christ—whom He did not raise up, if the dead do not rise" (vs. 15). Note that before he had said that the resurrection of Christ proves our own resurrection. But now he says that our resurrection will prove the truth of His; and truly both are true, for our rising is affirmed by Christ's rising. And His rising is demonstrated by ours.

(3) The denial of the resurrection also condemns those who have departed from this world in the faith of this doctrine. If Christ is not risen, then not only is your faith in vain, and not only are you still in your sins, but "then they who have fallen a-sleep in Christ have perished" (verse 18).

(4) He who denies the resurrection of the just concludes that the Christian is of all men the most miserable: "If in this life only we have hope in Christ, we are of all men most miserable" (vs.19). First we are most miserable of all men because we let go present enjoyments for those that will never come if the dead do not rise. We are most miserable because our faith and hope and joy and peace are all but a lie, if the dead do not rise. But you say that he who gives himself up to God shall have comfort in this life. Ah! but if the dead do not rise, all that comfort that we now think we have from God will then be found to be presumption and madness. Because we believe that God has so loved us as to have us in His day in body and soul to Heaven—which will not be so if the dead rise not. "We are of all men most miserable"—poor Christian! you that look for the blessed hope of the resurrection of the body at the glorious appearing of the great God and our Saviour Jesus Christ, how much you are deceived! if the dead rise not. "But now Christ has risen from the dead and has become the first fruits of those who slept. For since death came by man, the resurrection of the dead also came by man" (vs. 20,21).

(5) But again, he who denies the resurrection of the dead sets open a floodgate to all manner of impiety. He cuts the throat of a truly holy life and lays the reins upon the neck of the most outrageous lust. For if the dead do not rise, "Let us eat, drink and be merry, for tomorrow we die" (Isa. 22:13). Let us do anything ever so diabolical and hellish, if there is an end to us and if we shall not rise again to receive either good or evil.

(6) To deny this resurrection, even if a man but say it has al-

ready passed, his so saying tends directly to the destruction and overthrow of the faith of those that hear him. And it is so far from being according to the doctrine of God that it eats out good and wholesome doctrine even as cancer eats out the face and flesh of a man. How ugly do those look who have had their noses and lips eaten out with cancer! Even so ugly in the eyes of God and Christ is the teaching that there is no resurrection of the dead.

Lastly, I conclude that to deny the resurrection of the bodies of the just is to argue:

YOU HAVE GREAT IGNORANCE OF GOD! You are ignorant of His power to raise, ignorant of His promise to raise, ignorant of His faithfulness to raise. Therefore Paul says to those who were thus deluded, "Awaken to righteousness and sin not, for some do not have the knowledge of God. I speak this to your shame" (1 Cor. 15:34). As if he had said, Do you profess Christianity? And do you question the resurrection of the body? Do you not know that the resurrection of the body and the glory to follow is the very quintessence of the gospel of Jesus Christ? Are you ignorant of the resurrection of the Lord Jesus? And do you question the power and faithfulness of God, both to His Son and to His saints? You are ignorant of God, of what He can do, of what He will do, and of how He will glorify Himself by doing it.

YOU HAVE GROSS IGNORANCE OF THE TENOR AND CURRENT OF THE SCRIPTURES! For Christ said, "as regards the dead, that they rise, have you not read in the book of Moses how God spoke to him in the bush, saying, I am the God of Abraham and the God of Isaac and the God of Jacob? He is not the God of the dead, but the God of the living. Therefore you greatly err" (Mark 12:16,27). To be the God of Abraham, Isaac and Jacob is to be understood of His being their God under a new covenant relation, as He says, "I will be their God and they shall be My people"—so He is not the God of the dead, that is not of those that perish, whether they are angels or men.

Now I say that those who are the children of God are counted as living under a threefold consideration:

(1) They are living in their Lord and Head. And so all the elect may be said to live, for they are from eternity chosen in Him. He is their life, though possibly many of them are yet unconverted. Still I say that Christ is their life, by God's eternal purpose.

(2) The children of the new covenant do live. They live in their

spirits in glory by open vision; here they live by faith and the continual communication of grace from Christ into their souls.

(3) They live also with respect to their rising again, "f o r G o d c a l l s t h o s e t h i n g s t h a t a r e n o t a s t h o u g h t h e y w e r e" (Rom. 4:17). To be born, dead, buried, risen and ascended are all present with God,=He does not live by time, as we do. A thousand years to Him are but as the day that is past. Eternity, which is God Himself, does not admit of a first, a second, or a third. All things are naked and bare before Him and present with Him. All those that are His live unto Him.

There shall be a resurrection of the dead, both of the just and the unjust. A resurrection of what? of that which is sown, or of that which was never sown? If of that which is sown, then it must be either of that nature that was sown, or else of the corruption that cleaves to it. But it is the nature, not the corruption that cleaves to it, that rises again. And truly the very term 'resurrection' is a forcible argument to prove that the dead shall come forth out of their graves—for the Holy Spirit has always spoken more properly than to say "t h e r e s h a l l b e a r e s u r r e c t i o n o f t h e d e a d , b o t h o f t h e j u s t a n d t h e · u n j u s t" (Acts 24:15), when yet neither the good nor the bad shall come forth out of their graves, but rather something else to delude the world.

THE MANNER OF THE RISING OF THE JUST

So, having in a few words shown you the truth of the resurrection of the dead, I now come to the manner of their rising.

And first of the rising of those who are called the just.

When the apostle had proven the truth and certainty of the resurrection in 1 Cor. 15, he descends to the discovery of the manner of it. And that he might remove those foolish scruples that attend the hearts of the ignorant, he begins with one of their questions: "B u t s o m e w i l l s a y , H o w a r e t h e d e a d r a i s e d u p , a n d w i t h w h a t b o d y d o t h e y c o m e ?" (1 Cor. 15:35). To which he answers first by a similitude of sead that is sown in the earth. In this similitude he inserts three things:

(1) Our reviving or rising must be after death, "T h a t w h i c h i s s o w n i s n o t m a d e a l i v e u n l e s s i t d i e s" (verse 36).

(2) Then at our rising we shall not only revive and live, but we shall be changed into a far more glorious state than when we were sown, "t h a t w h i c h y o u s o w — y o u d o n o t s o w t h a t b o d y t h a t s h a l l b e" — "B u t G o d g i v e s i t a b o d y a s i t h a s p l e a s e d H i m" (vs. 37,38). That is, He gives the body more

splendor, more lustre, more beauty at its resurrection.

(3) But neither its being made alive, nor yet its transcendent splendor shall hinder it from being the same body (as to the nature of it) that was sown in the earth. For as God gives it a body for honor and splendor, as it pleases Him, so "to every seed its own body" (verse 38, end).

And indeed this similitude by which he here reasons the manner of the resurrection of the just is very natural and fits each part-icular. For as to its burial, (1) the corn of wheat is first dead, and afterward sown and buried in the earth—so is the body of man. (2) After the seed is thus dead and buried, then it comes alive and revives. So shall it also be with our body. For after it is laid in the grave and buried, it shall come alive, rise and revive.

Again, as to the manner of its change in its rising, this simili-tude also is fitted, as (1) It is sown a dead seed; it is raised a living one. (2) It is sown dry and without beauty; it rises green and beaut-iful. (3) It is sown a single seed, it rises a full ear. (4) It is sown in its husk, but in its rising it leaves the husk behind it.

Further, though the kernel thus die, is buried, and meets with all this change and alteration in these things, yet none of them can cause the nature of the kernel to cease—it is still wheat! Wheat was sown and wheat rises. Only it is sown dead, dry and barren wheat, but it rises living, beautiful and fruitful wheat. It has this alteration then, that it greatly changes its resemblance—but it has this power also, that it still retains its own nature (1 Cor. 15:38).

The apostle having thus presented the manner of the resurrect-ion of the saints, by the nature of seed sown and rising again, he proceeds to three more similitudes for further illustration: (1) to show us the variety and glory of flesh; (2) to show us the dif-ference between the glory that is between heavenly bodies and those that are earthly; (3) to show us the difference that is between the glory of the light of the sun and the glory of the light of the moon.

As if he should say, At the resurrection of the bodies, they will be more abundantly altered and changed than if the flesh of beasts and fowls were made as noble as the flesh of men; or the bodies of earth were made as excellent as the heavenly bodies; or as if the glory of the moon should be made as bright and as clear as the glory of the sun; or as if the glory of the least star was as glorious as the biggest star in the expanse of Heaven.

It is a resurrection indeed, a resurrection in every way. The body arises as to the nature of it, the self-same nature. But as to the manner of it, how far transcendent it is! There is a poor, dry, wrinkled kernel cast into the ground, and there it lies and swells and breaks. And one would think that it would perish. But behold, it receives life and begins to rise, then to put forth a blade, then grows a stalk and an ear, then it blossoms into a full kernel in the ear. It is the same wheat, yet behold how the form and fashion of that which now arises differs from that which was sown. Also, its glory when sown is no glory at all when compared with that in which it arises. Yet it is the same that rises as was sown, not another. Though now it is the same in a far more glorious manner, not having the husk any more, for our bran will be left behind us when we rise again.

The comparison between the heavenly bodies and the earthly bodies also holds forth the same. "The glory of the heavenly is truly different, and that of the earthly is different" (1 Cor. 15:40). Now note that he does not speak here of the natures of each of these bodies, but of the glory that one has above another. The glory of the heavenly is one, and the glory of the earthly is another. Therefore when we rise we shall not change our nature, I say, but our glory. We shall be equal to the angels, not as regards their nature, but as regards their glory.

A beggar has the same nature as a king. Gold in the ore has the same nature as that which is most refined. But the beggar does not have the same glory as the king, and gold in the ore does not have the same glory as that which is much refined. Yet our state when we arise out of the heart of the earth will be far more altered than any of these, being like so many suns in the heavens.

Consideration of these things shows the vanity of those arguments which say that our human nature consists of body and soul and shall not inherit the kingdom of God. We also see how far from their purpose is that saying of the apostle, "flesh and blood shall not inherit the kingdom of God" (1 Cor. 15:50). Rather, dear reader, consider that frequently in Scripture the words "flesh and blood" is not to be understood of that matter which God made (such as flesh which cleaves to our bones, and the blood that runs in our veins,) but it is taken for that corruption, weakness, mortality and evil which clings to human nature. This weakness and corruption possessing all men also wholly rules the unconverted soul. Therefore it bears the name of that which it rules, that which is actuated by it, namely, our whole man, consisting of body and soul. Yet I say that it is a distinct thing from that flesh and blood which is essential to our being, without which we are not men.

In Galatians 5:24, Paul writes, "They that are Christ's crucified the flesh with its passions and lusts". Who is so vain as to think that the apostle means that our material flesh, that which hangs on our bones and is mixed with our blood, is crucified? But rather he means that inward fountain of sin, corruption and wickedness, "the old man" with his "deceitful lusts' is crucified. Again, "the flesh lusts against the Spirit, and the Spirit against the flesh" (Gal. 5:17) Is this our flesh that hangs on our bones which lusts against the Spirit? If this is so, then it is our duty not to nourish it, for then we would be nourishing that which fights against the Spirit of God. Nay, if the Spirit lusts against the flesh which is on our bones, then it is our duty to destroy it with all speed. But rather we know that "flesh" here is to be understood of the corrupt apprehension and wisdom, with those inclinations to evil that lodge within us.

Observe that all these places point to a corrupt soul rather than a corrupt body. For truly sin and all spiritual wickednesses have their seat in the heart and soul of a man, and it is by using this or that member of the body that they defile a man. Therefore, where you read of flesh and blood being rejected by God, especially when it speaks of the flesh and blood of saints, you are not to understand it as meant of the flesh which is proper to the body. But it is that weakness which cleaves to the soul since the Fall.

Further, as regards our real substantial flesh, it may be considered as the creation of God purely, or it may be considered as being corrupted by sin. Now if it is corrupted, it shall not inherit the kingdom of God. But considered as God's creation, all that God has converted to Himself through Jesus Christ shall when changed inherit the kingdom of God, even the body. The woman whose clothes are dirty can tell the difference between the dirt and the cloth. So God deals with us in cleansing our body. It is true that there is not a saint that is not infected with many corrupt and filthy things and many sinful infirmities, because of that body of sin and death that yet remains in us. But still God distinguishes between our weaknesses and His workmanship. He knows how to save the whole man while He is destroying the corruption and weakness that clings to it.

Therefore that Scripture, "flesh and blood shall not inherit the kingdom of God" cannot be understood to mean that flesh which is man's nature cannot enter God's kingdom. For then Christ would lose His members, the purchase of His blood, the vessels and temples of His Spirit, for all this is our body.

Then, too, Christ in that body of His, which is also our flesh and blood, is not in glory, which is contrary to the current of the New Testament. Yes, it would be nonsense to say that there would be a resurrection and that our vile body would be changed and made like the body of the Son of God, if it is not this body which rises but some other thing which is not now in us and our nature.

But the apostle here is speaking properly of that mortality and weakness which now attends our whole man, not of our real substantial body itself. For after he had said, "flesh and blood shall not inherit the kingdom of God" he adds, "nor does rottenness inherit purity" (1 Cor. 15:50). These two sayings answer to what he presently adds, saying, "Behold! I tell you a heavenly secret: We shall not all fall asleep, but we shall all be changed—in an instant, in the twinkling of an eye, at the last trumpet. For a trumpet shall sound and the dead shall be raised forever pure, and we shall be changed" (vss 51,52). Mark it, the DEAD shall be raised incorruptible. For "this corruptible must put on incorruption and this mortal shall put on immortality." It is this corruptible, I say, and this mortal, that must be raised (though it is buried corruptible and mortal, it is raised immortal and incorruptible). It shall leave its grave-clothes of sinful corruption and mortality behind it.

The manner of this rising is more distinctly brought out by the apostle in four particulars:
1. The body is "sown in corruption, raised in incorruption."
2. It is "sown in dishonor, it is raised in glroy."
3. It is "sown in weakness, it is raised in power."
4. It is "sown a natural body, it is raised a spiritual body."

1. "It is raised in incorruption" (vs. 42).

We are brought into this world by sin and corruption. Corruption is our father, and our mother conceives us in sin. And thus we have our lives attended with vanity and vexation of spirit. But now being raised from the dead in an incorruptible state, those things that annoy us in this life and which take away that life are effectually destroyed. And therefore we live forever, as the Spirit says in Revelation 21:4.

In our resurrection there shall be no corruption either of the body or of the soul; no weakness or sickness, etc. Therefore when he says, "It is raised in incorruption," it is as if he had said, "it is impossible that we should ever sin anymore, be sick anymore, sorrow anymore, or die anymore." Those that are counted worthy of that world cannot "die anymore, for they are equal to the angels and are the children of God, being the children of the resurrection" (Luke 20:36).

2. "It is raised in GLORY" (vs. 43).

The dishonor that attends the saint at his departing from this world is often very great. He is sown "in dishonor". Some are hanged, some are starved, some are torn in pieces, not even being put into graves. But "it is raised in glory" Glory is the sweetness, purity and perfection of a thing. Therefore to rise in glory is first to arise in all the beauty and utmost completeness that a human body may possess. I say that in all its features and members it is inconceivably beautiful. Sin and corruption have made sad work of our bodies, as well as of our souls. It is sin that is the common cause of deformity, that which makes us so dishonorable at our death. But at our resurrection, being raised incorruptible, we shall appear in such perfections of all sorts that all the beauty and sweetness and amiableness that ever may have been in this world shall be swallowed up a thousand times with this new glory.

The Psalmist says of Christ that He is "fairer than the children of men" (Psalm 45:2). I believe that in His outward man as well as in His inward parts He was the purest and most beautiful man that God ever made until "His visage was marred more than any man" (Isa. 52:14), by His persecutors —for in all things He had and will have the pre-eminence. Now our bodies at our resurrection will not only be as free from sin as His was before He died, but also as free from all other infirmities as He was after He was raised again. In a word, if incorruptibleness can put a beauty upon our bodies when they arise, then we shall have it. There will be no lame legs, no crumpled shoulders, nor any bleary eyes and wrinkled faces. For our Lord Jesus Christ "will completely transform our body (in which we are now humbled), for it to be made like His glorious body—according to the almighty working of His power," (Philippians 4:21).

Again, all the glory that a glorified soul can help this body to gain will be possessed at that time. That soul which has been all these years resting in the bosom of Christ will in a moment come into the body again, inhabiting every member of it as it did before its departure. The Spirit of God also will not dwell in this body again in all perfection. The body at that day will shine brighter than Moses' face, as bright as the sun and the stars and the angels. "When Christ, our life, shall appear, then shall you also appear with Him in glory" (Colossians 3:4).

3. "It is raised in POWER" (vs. 43).

While we are here we are attended with so many weaknesses and infirmities that in time the least sin or sickness is too hard for us. Our strength, our beauty, our days, our breath and life are in time taken away because of our weakness. But, behold! We are raised in power! And it will be such power that all these things here below will be as a grasshopper appears to a giant—the gates of death and the bars of the grave will be carried away on our shoulders, as Samson carried away the gates of the city. We shall then carry that grace, majesty, terror and commanding power in our souls that will make our faces like lightning. Then "shall be brought to pass the saying that has been written, Death is swallowed up in victory" (vs. 54).

4. "It is raised a SPIRITUAL body" (vs. 44).

This is the last particular and is indeed the reason of the others. It is an incorruptible body because it is a spiritual body. It is a glorious body because it is a spiritual body. It rises in power because it is a spiritual body. When the body is buried in the earth, it is a corruptible body, dishonorable, weak and natural. When it rises, it rises incorruptible, glorious, powerful and spiritual. So as far as incorruption is above corruption, glory above dishonor, power above weakness, and spiritual is above nature, so great a change will be in our body when it is raised again. And yet it is this body, not another; it is in this nature, though changed into a far more glorious state.

Not that "it is sown a natural body". Though ever so much of the Spirit and grace of God may dwell in it while it lives, as soon as the soul is separated from it, then also the Spirit of God separates from it, and it will continue so until its resurrection. Therefore it is laid into the earth a mere lump of man's nature. "It is sown a natural body" but at that day when "the heavens shall be no more" then the trumpet shall sound and, in a moment, the dead shall be raised incorruptible, glorious and spiritual. So then the body when it rises will be so swallowed up by life and immortality that it will be as if it had lost its own human nature. But, in truth, the same substantial real nature is every whit there still. It is the same "it" that rises that was sown, "it" is sown, "it" is raised, the apostle says.

If we lost our proper human nature, then, we would lose our very being, we would be annihilated. But Christ has shown us what our body at the resurrection shall be like, by showing us what His body was like after His resurrection. We read that His body retained the very same flesh and bones that hung upon the cross, yet how angelical it was! He could come in to His disciples with that very body when the doors were shut upon them. He could at pleasure appear in the twinkling of an eye in the midst of them. He could be visible and invisible, as He pleased. In a word, He could pass and repass, ascend and descend in that body, with far more pleasure and ease than the bird on the wing.

Now as we have in this world borne the image of our first father, so at that day we shall have the image of Jesus Christ and be as He is. "Even as we bore the image of the one made of dust, so we shall also bear the image of the Heavenly One" (vs. 48). He shall "change our vile body so that it may be made like His glorious body" (Phil. 3:21). How? Mark it, "according to the almighty working of His power, even to put all things under Himself" (same). As if He should say, I know that there are many things that in this world hinder us from having our bodies like the body of Christ, but when God shall raise us from the dead, we will then have bodies like those of His Son, and He will then have such a power working on and in our body as to remove all hindrances.

Further this body, being thus spiritualized, shall be infinitely enlarged in all its faculties. We "shall see Him as He is" and "we shall know, even as we are known."

First, we shall see Christ in His glory, not only by revelation as we do now. Then we shall see Him face to face and we will be with Him to the end. Then we shall see into all things. There shall not be anything hidden from us. There shall not be a saint, a prophet, any saved soul but we shall then perfectly know them. We shall also know the works of creation, election and redemption. We shall see and know as thoroughly the things of heaven, earth and hell as we now know our ABC's. For the Spirit with which we shall be filled, He that searches all things, yea, the deep things of God, will then teach us.

Though God's saints have felt the power of much of His grace and have had many a sweet word fulfilled upon them, yet one word will be unfulfilled on their particular persons as long as the grave can close its mouth upon them. But, as I said before, when the gates of death open before them and the bars of the grave fall apart, then shall be brought to pass that saying which is written, *"death is swallowed up in victory"*.

Now you must know that the time of the rising of the just will be at the coming of the Lord. For when they are to rise, the Lord Jesus Christ will appear in the clouds in flaming fire, with all His mighty angels. And the effect of this appearing will be the rising of the dead. "For the Lord Himself shall come down from Heaven with a shout, with the voice of the archangel and with the trumpet of God. And the dead in Christ shall rise first" (1 Thess. 4:16).

At the time of the Lord's coming, there will be found alive both saints and sinners. As for the saints then alive, they shall not die. But as soon as all the saints are raised out of their graves, changed and swallowed up by incorruption, immortality and glory, then those yet alive will have the same spiritual translation as the dead in Christ have just experienced. As Paul says, "We shall not all sleep, but we shall all be changed in a moment ...for the trumpet shall sound and the dead shall be raised incorruptible, and we shall be changed" (1 Cor. 15:52). And again, in 1 Thess. 4:17, "Then those who are left alive shall be caught up together with them in the clouds to meet the Lord in the air. And so we shall always be with the Lord". And He also says in another place, "I therefore call upon you in the sight of God and the Lord Jesus Christ who shall judge the living and the dead at His appearing" (2 Timothy 4:1).

Now when the saints that sleep shall be raised thus incorruptible, powerful, glorious and spiritual, and those who are found alive are made like them, then immediately—before the unjust are raised,— the saints shall appear before the judgment seat of the Lord Jesus Christ. There they shall give an account to their Lord, the judge of all things they have done. And there they shall receive a reward according to the good which they have done.

They shall arise before the wicked are raised, they being the proper children of the resurrection. Therefore it is said that when they arise, it is a rising from the dead—that is, their rising is a leaving of the reprobate world behind them. And it must be so because also the saints will have done their accounting and will be set upon the throne with Christ as kings and princes with Him to judge the world when the wicked are raised. The saints "shall judge the world" and shall even "judge angels". Yea, the·
-26-

shall sit upon the throne of judgment to do it.

Now when the saints are raised, they must give an account of all things that they have done while they were in the world, of all things, "whether they were good or bad."

1. They must give account of all that was BAD.

But mark that they are not appearing as vagabond slaves and sinners, but as sons and stewards, as servants of the Lord Jesus. This is taught by different places in the Holy Scriptures. First, Paul says, "We must all stand before the judgment seat of Christ" (Rom. 14:10). That is, we who are saints. For it is written, "I live, says the Lord, so that every knee shall bow to Me and every tongue shall confess to God. So then each of us shall give account of himself to God" (Romans 14:11,12).

Again, "We must all appear before the judgment seat of Christ—so that each one may receive the things done in the body, according to what he did, whether good or evil" (2 Cor. 5:10).

It is true that God loves His people, but He does not love their sins, nor does He love anything they do that is contrary to His word. Therefore, as surely as God will give a reward to His saints and children, for all that they have truly done well—so truly He will at this day distinguish their good and bad deeds. And when both are manifested by the righteous judgment of Christ, He will burn up their bad works, with all their labor, travail and pains in it forever. He knows how to save His people and still take vengeance on their evil inventions.

Now observe in 1 Corinthians 3:12-15 that (1) Christ is the foundation; (2) the gold, silver and precious stones that are said to be built on Him are all the actings in faith and love according to the word which the saints are found doing for His sake in the world. And, (3), to build on Him wood, hay and stubble is to build together with what is human inventions and carnal ordinances, fathering them upon God and His allowance. (4), the fire that you read of is the pure word and law of God. (5), the day you read of is the day of Christ's coming to judgment to reveal the hidden things of darkness, to make manifest the counsels of the heart. (6), At this day the gold, silver, precious stones, wood, hay and stubble of every man shall be tried by this fire, the word, that it may be known what sort it is.

Observe again, (1) that the apostle speaks here of the saved, not of the reprobates: "he himself shall be saved" (vs. 15). (2), this saved man may have wood, hay and stubble; that is, things that will not abide the trial. (3), neither this man's goodness, nor yet God's love toward him, shall hinder all his wood, hay or stubble from being made manifest, for "the fire shall try every man's work, what kind it is" (vs. 13). (4), so a good man will see all his wood, hay and stubble burned up in the trial before his face. (5), that good man will then suffer loss, the loss of all things that were not done according to the word of God.

It must be unavoidably concluded that the whole body of the elect must account for all things they have done, whether good or bad. And it must be that He will destroy all their bad with the purity of His word. Yea, and all their pains, travail and labor which they spent about it shall be for nought. There are now many things done by the best of the saints which will then be gladly disowned by them, yea, they will be ashamed of the things they have done with great devotion. Alas! What gross things some of the saints father upon God, counting Him to be author of them and the promotor of them. Yes, and as they father many superstitions and Scripture-less things upon Him, so they die in the same opinion, never coming to the sight of their evil and ignorance in them. But now the judgment day is the time when everything shall be set in its proper place. That which is of God will be in one place, that which is not of God will be revealed and made plain. "In many things now we all offend" (James 3:2). Then we shall see the many offences we have committed and shall ourselves judge them.

The Christian even in this world, when he is not under some great temptation, will confess to his God before all men, telling how he has sinned and transgressed against his Father. He will fall down at the feet of God and cry out, "I have sinned." And if the Christian is so simple and open-hearted with God in the days of his imperfection, even though accompanied with many infirmities and temptations, then how much more freely will he confess and acknowledge his miscarriages when he comes before the Lord and Saviour absolutely stripped of all temptation and imperfection! At the judgment seat every knee shall bow and reverence God the Creator, even Christ the Redeemer of the world. And every tongue shall confess to God that only His will should have been obeyed in all things by them, and the saints will most naturally and freely admit in how many things they were deceived, mistaken, deluded, and drawn aside from their intention to honor and glorify God.

But yet take notice that in that day, when the saints are accounting for their evil before their Saviour and Judge, they will not upon such remembrance and confession of sin be filled with guilt, confusion and shame that now attends their souls. Nor shall they be grieved or offended because God has laid bare to the last tittle their sins and weaknesses even before the angels.

For, (1), they will see now more perfectly than ever that God loves them and forgives them all even before they confess to Him. And they shall have their souls so full of the ravishing rapture of the life and glory that they are in that they shall be swallowed up in such a way as to chase away fear and guilt and confusion. Their Judge is their Saviour, their husband and head. And though He will bring them to judgment for all their evil deeds, yet He will keep them forever out of condemnation; "P e r f e c t l o v e c a s t s o u t f e a r" even now in this life, much more then when we are with our Saviour, having passed from death unto life.

(2), the saints at that day shall have their hearts and souls so wrapped up in the pleasure of God their Saviour that ti will be their delight to see all things which were not according to His word and will to perish. When we come into His presence, we will delight in the very perfection of delight to see His will done.

(3), but the reason for the account of the saints at the day of God will be not only the vindication of the righteousness, holiness and purity of the word, nor will it center only in the revealing of the knowledge and heart-discerning nature of Christ—but it also is for the purpose of setting off and heighthening of their apprehensions of the tender affection which God has for them. The sight of their sin and vanity will also increase their joy and sweetness of soul, will cause them to cling with their hearts unto their God. Even while here, saints come to know that a sense of their sin and the assurance of God's pardon will do marvelous work in their poor hearts. What meltings of heart do we have without a sense of our guilt? What humility do we have without being cast down? Does not the sense of sin work in the soul of the creature to see its nothingness? The sweetest frame, the most heart-endearing frame that a Christian can possibly get into while still in this world is to have a warm sight of sin, and at the same time a clear view of his Saviour, upon the heart all at one time. O then it will weep, not because of fear, but by the constraining grace and mercy of God, the Saviour. And at this very time it is so far from being disquieted because of the sight of its wickedness, that it is driven into an ecstasy because of the love and mercy which it can see mingled with the sense of sin in the soul. This is the time when the heart sees the most of the power of mercy, the virtue and the value, the excellency of Christ in all His offices. It is then that Christ comes to be glorified in and by His saints.

Therefore, though the saints receive by faith the forgiveness of sins in this life, and so have passed from death to life, yet again, Christ Jesus and God the Father will have every one of these sins reckoned up again and brought fresh upon the stage in the day of judgment, so that they may see and be sensible forever what grace and mercy they have experienced. And this I take to be the reason for that remarkable saying of the apostle Peter, "Therefore repent and be converted, for the blotting out of your sins, so that the times of refreshing from the presence of the Lord may come" (Acts 3:19). If a sense of some sin (for who sees all?) and a sight of the love of God will here work upon the spirit of the godly to melt them, then what will a sight of all their sin do, when together with it they are personally present with their Lord and Saviour?

Yes, if a sight of some sins, with a possibility of pardon, will make the heart love, reverence, fear, with guiltless and heart-affecting fears, then what will a general sight of all his sins, and together with them an eternal acquittance from them, work on the heart of a saint forever! O the wisdom and goodness of God, that He at this day should so turn about the worst of our things (even those that naturally sink us and damn us) for our great advantage! All things shall work together for good, indeed, to those that love God. Those sins that brought a curse upon the whole world, that spilled the blood of our dear Saviour and laid His tender soul under the flaming wrath of God, shall by God's wisdom and love tend to the exaltation of His grace and the inflaming of our affections toward Him forever and ever.

It will not be so with reprobates! It will not be so with devils! It is only the saved who have this privilege peculiar to themselves. Why, then, does God let saints also make that advantage of their sin, that they glorify God thereby? It is not that we may say, "Let us do evil that good may come," or, "Let us sin so that grace may abound". But it is by taking occasion by the sin that is already past that we set the crown upon the head of Christ for our justification. We continually look upon it so as to press close to the Lord Jesus for grace and mercy through Him, so that we may be kept humble forever under His dispensations.

2. Having accounted for all their evil and confessed to God's glory as to how they fell short, not doing the truth in this or that particular, and having received their eternal acquittance from the Lord and Judge in the sight of both angels and saints, the Lord Jesus will immediately make inquiry into all their GOOD DEEDS.

Now at this time all things shall be reckoned, from the very first good thing that was done by Adam or Abel, to the last that will be done in the world. Also at this time all the good deeds of masters of families, of parents, of children, of servants, of neighbors, or whatever good things anyone has done, shall be revealed.

(1) There will be a reward for all that have sincerely labored in the word and doctrine; rewards for all the souls they have saved by their word, and for all those watered by the same. It is here that Paul the planter, and Apollos the waterer, with every one of their companions shall receive the reward according to their works. It is here that all the preaching, praying, watching and labor which you have bestowed in trying to catch men away from Satan and take them to God, I say it is here they shall be rewarded with glory. Every soul you have converted to the Lord Jesus, that you have comforted, that you have helped by good counsel or admonition, shall stick as a pearl in that crown which the Lord, the righteous Judge, shall give you at that day. That is, of course, if you have done it willingly, delighting to lift up the name of God among men. If you have done it with love and longing for the salvation of sinners, you shall be rewarded—otherwise you shall have only your pains, and no more. As the apostle Paul said, If I do this willingly I have a reward; but if against my will, then a dispensation of the gospel is committed to my charge.

But I say, If you do it graciously, then a reward will follow. "For what is our hope, our joy, our crown of rejoicing? ...you are our glory and joy" (1 Thess. 2:19,20). Let him, therefore, that Christ has put into His harvest take comfort in the midst of all his sorrow and know that God acknowledges that anyone who converts a sinner from the error of his way saves that soul from death and covers a multitude of sins. Therefore labor to convert, labor to water, labor to build up, labor to feed the flock of God which is among you, taking the oversight of it, not by constraint, but willingly—not for filthy lucre, but of a ready mind, "And when the chief Shepherd has been revealed, you shall receive the crown of glory that never fades away" (1 Peter 5:4).

(2) And as the minister of Christ's gospel shall at this day be rewarded, so shall those more private saints be looked upon with tender affections and love, and they shall be rewarded for all their work and labor of love, which they have shown toward the name of Christ, in ministering to His saints and suffering for His sake. "knowing that whatever good each man may have done, he shall receive this from the Lord," (Eph.

6:8). Ah! Little do the people of God think how largely and thoroughly God will at that Day own and reward all the good and holy acts of
His people. Every bit, every drop, every rag, shall be rewarded in
that Day before men and angels—"whoever shall give to one
of these little ones only a cup of cold water to
drink, in the name of a disciple, truly I say to
you, he shall in no way lose his reward!" (Matt. 10:42).
"When you make a feast, call the poor, maimed,
lame, and blind—and you shall be blessed; for they
have nothing to repay you. It shall be repaid to
you in the resurrection of the just" (Luke 14:13).

If there is any repentance among the godly at this Day, it will
be because the Lord Jesus, in His person, members and word was
not confessed, honored and served by them when they were in this
world. For it will be ravishing to all when they see what notice the
Lord Jesus will then take of every widow's mite. He will even call
to mind all those acts of mercy and kindness which you have shown
to Him when you were among men. He will remember and will proclaim before angels those aces of yours which you have either forgotten or in humility will not at that Day count worthy of owning.
He will count them up so fast and so fully that you will cry out,
Lord, when did I do this? And when did I do that? "When did we
see You hungry and fed You? or thirsty and gave
You drink? etc." (Matt. 25:37-40). And the King will answer
"It was when you did it to the least of My brothers that you have
done it to Me. The good works of some are plainly seen beforehand,
and those that are otherwise cannot be hidden. Whatever you have
done to one of the least of these, you have done it to Me. I felt the
nourishment of your food, the warmth of your fleece; I remember
your loving and holy visits to My members who were sick, and in
prison, and the like. When they were strangers and wanderers in
the world, you took them in. "Well done, good and faithful servant: enter into the joy of your Lord."

(3) There will also be a reward here for all that suffering, that
enduring of affliction that you have met with for your Lord. Now
Christ will begin from the greatest suffering and continue down
to the least, and He will bestow a reward on all of them—from
the blood of the suffering saint down to the loss of a hair, nothing
shall go unrewarded. "For I reckon that the sufferings
of this present time are not worthy to be compared with the glory about to be revealed to us"
(Romans 8:18). Behold by the Scriptures how God has recorded

the sufferings of His people, and also how He has promised to reward them, "Blessed are you when they shall call you names, and shall persecute, and lying shall say every evil word against you for My sake. Rejoice and leap for joy! for great is your reward in Heaven"(Matt. 5:11). "And everyone who has left houses, or brothers, or sisters, or father, or mother, or wife, or children, or lands, for the sake of My name, shall receive a hundredfold and shall inherit everlasting life"(Matthew 19:29).

(4) There will also be a reward at this Day for all the more retired works, the more secret deeds of Christianity. (A) There is not now one single act of faith in the soul which shall not in that Day be found out and praised, honored, glorified, in the face of Heaven. (B) There is not one groan unto God in secret against your lusts, or for more grace, light, spirit, sanctification or strength to go through this world like a Christian, which shall not be openly rewarded at the coming of Christ. (C) Not a single tear has dropped from your tender eye against your lusts, the love of this world, or for more communion with Jesus Christ, but (as it is now in the bottle of God) then it shall bring forth such plenty of reward that it will return upon you with abundance of increase. "Those who sow in tears shall reap in joy. He who goes forth and weeps, bearing precious seed, shall doubtless come again with rejoicing, bringing his sheaves with him" (Psalm 126:5,6).

WHAT REWARD SHALL BE GIVEN THE SAINTS?

Having in brief shown you something concerning the resurrection of the saints, and that they shall account with their Lord at His coming (both for the burning up of what was not according to the truth, and in rewarding them for all their good,) it remains that I now show you something also of that with which they shall be rewarded.

1. Then those that are found in the day of their resurrection to have their good things brought upon the state, they that then shall be found to be the people who labored most for God while here, these shall at that Day enjoy the greatest portion of God. It is they that shall be possessed with most of the glory of the Godhead then, for that is the portion of the saints in general. And why should he who does most for God in this world enjoy most of Him in that which is to come? It is because this doing and acting of the heart for God enlarges every faculty of the soul, giving it

more capacity, making more room in the soul for glory! Every vessel
of glory shall at that Day be full of glory. But not every vessel
will be able to contain the same measure of glory. For some, if
it is poured upon them, will not be able to stand under it (for there
is an eternal weight in the glory that saints shall there enjoy (2
Cor. 4:17), and every vessel must be filled at that Day, receiving
its heavenly load.

All Christians do not have the same enjoyment of God in this life.
And if they had it, they would not be equally able to bear it. But
those Christians that are most laborious for God in this world,
these already have the most of Him in their souls. And it is not
only because diligence in God's ways is the means by which God
communicates Himself, but it is also because the senses are made
more strong and able to understand God by being used, thus they
become able to discern both good and evil. For he that has, to him
shall more be given, and he shall have it more abundantly. He who
has laid out his pound for his master, who has gained then with it,
he shall be made ruler over ten cities. But he who gained but five
shall be given only five. In this life, he who is best bred and nourished in his youth is best able to manage when he is a man (as regards the things of this life). But always he who is best bred and
nourished in the bosom of God, he who acts for Him while here, is
the man that will be best able to enjoy most of God in the kingdom
of Heaven. Paul tells us, "our affliction..is working out
for us a far more excellent eternal weight of
glory" (2 Cor. 4:17). Our afflictions do it. But not only is it because there is a reward laid up for the afflicted, according to the
degree of affliction, but because affliction and every other service toward God makes the heart more deep, more practiced, more
knowing. So it is more able to hold and to bear more of God.

And this is the very reason for such sayings as these: "Urge
them to do good, to be rich in good works, to be ready to give, ready
to share in fellowship, treasuring up for themselves a good foundation for the time to come, so that they may lay hold on everlasting life" (1 Tim. 6:19). Now that eternal life is not the matter of
our justification from sin in the sight of God, for that is done
freely by grace through faith in Christ's blood. But here the a-
postle is speaking of the same things which in the other place is
said to bring a far more exceeding eternal weight of glory. In stir-
ring them up to be diligent in good works, he tells us it is because
he wants us to have fruit that will abound to our account (Phil.
4:17). As he says in 1 Cor. 15:58, "be firm, so that you can-

not be moved, abounding in the work of the Lord always, knowing that your labor is not in vain in the Lord" (1 Corinthians 15:58).

Therefore I say that the reward which the saints shall have at that Day, for all the good which they have done, is going to be the enjoyment of God according to their works (though they shall be freely justified and glorified without works).

2. As the enjoyment of God at that Day will be to the saints in accordance with their works and doings (again, I do not speak now of justification from sin), so their praise and commendation at that Day shall also be according to their works, with both being their degrees of glory. For as God by communicating Himself to us at that Day will thereby glorify us, so He also will cause to be proclaimed in the presence of all the holy angels everything that has been done by us for God, for His people, while we have been here. "everyone who shall confess Me before men, I will also confess him before My Father who is in Heaven" (Matthew 10:32).

Now when Christ comes in His glory those of whom He is ashamed will lie under inconceivable disgrace, shame, dishonor, contempt. So those who have pleased Christ shall be confessed by Him, owned, honored, commended and praised at that Day. For then "shall every man have praise of God" namely, according to his works. Christ then shall proclaim before you and all others what you have done, what you have suffered, what you have confessed, and what you have stood for His name. "This is the man," He will say, "that overcame the flatteries, the threats, the allurements and the enticings of a whole world for Me! Behold him, he is an Israelite indeed."

When King Ahasuerus became aware of the good service which Mordecai had done toward him, then he commanded that the royal apparel and the crown, together with the horse that the king rode upon, should be given to Mordecai, and he commanded that he should be led through the city in the presence of all his nobles, arrayed with the crown, dressed in the apparel, and riding the horse of the king. And he commanded that a proclamation should be made before him, "This is what shall be done to the man whom the king delights to honor" (Esther 6:9). In this way Ahasuerus was a type to hold forth to the children of God how kindly God will take all their labor and service of love to Him, and how He will honor and dignify those who do so. The meaning of the parable in Luke 12, verses 35, 36, is this, that those souls that shall make it their business to honor the Lord Jesus Christ in the day of their temptation may be sure that He will make it His business to honor and glorify them in the day of His glorification: "If anyone serves Me, the Father will honor him" (John 12:26). It has been God's way in this world to proclaim the acts and doings of His saints in His word, before all the world, and He will do it in that world to come also.

3. There is another thing that shall still be added to the glory of the saints in the kingdom of their Saviour, at His coming. It is this, that each of them shall then have his throne and place of degree on Christ's right hand and on His left, in His glorious kingdom. For as Christ will have a special eye on us and a tender and affectionate heart to reward to the full every good thing that any have done for His name in the world, so also He will have as great regard that there be a place and state that is fitting for every member of his body. When the mother of James and John petitioned our Saviour to grant that her two sons might sit one on His right hand and one on His left hand in His kingdom, though He did not grant her this request, yet He affirmed that there would be places of degrees and honor in Heaven, "to sit at My right hand and at My left hand is not Mine to give; but to those for whom it has been prepared" (Mark 10:40).

In the Temple there were rooms bigger and smaller, higher and lower, more inward and more outward. These rooms were types of the places which our Lord told us He went to prepare for us (John 14:2). In this world, the foot shall not have the place prepared for the eye, nor yet the hand have that which is prepared for the ear; even so everyone shall have his own place in the body of Christ, and he shall have the glory also prepared for such a relation. It is comely to have order in earth, so much more the God of order shall have order in Heaven, where all things shall be done in their utmost perfections. Enoch, Noah, Abraham, Moses, Joshua, David, Solomon, all the prophets, shall each have his place, according to the degree of Old Testament saints. As God said to Daniel, "go your way until the end. For you shall rest and stand in your lot at the end of the days" (Daniel 14:13). And Peter, Paul, Timothy, and all the other church-officers, have their place and heavenly state, according as God has set them in the Church in the New Testament.

Having gone thus far, I shall now come to the second part of the text, that there shall be a resurrection of THE WICKED: "There shall be a resurrection of the dead, both of the just and the UNJUST" (Acts 24:15).

For as the just go before the unjust in name, in dignity, and in honor, so they shall in the last day go before them in the resurrection. When the saints have risen out of their graves, have given up their accounts to God, have received their glory and have been set upon their thrones, when all of them are arrayed in royal apparel, having donned their crowns of glory—then the unjust shall come out of their graves to receive their judgment for what they have done in the body. As Paul says, "For we all must appear before the judgment seat of Christ—so that each one may receive the things done in the body, according to what he did, whether good or evil"(2 Corinthians 5:10).

But because I do not desire for others to receive for a truth anything unless I have proven it by the word of God, I therefore shall prove the resurrection of the wicked:

1. First, then, it is evident that the wicked shall rise from the very names and terms that the raised shall then go under—these are the very same names that they went under when they lived in this world. They are called the heathen, the nations, the world, the wicked, and, those that do iniquity. They are called men, women, Sodom, Sidon, etc. "it shall be more tolerable for Sodom in the Day of judgment" than for other sinners. "But the heavens and the earth which now exist are kept by the same word, being kept for fire unto the Day of judgment and destruction of ungodly men"(2 Peter 3:7). Now these terms, or names, are not given to the spirits of the wicked only, but is given to them as consisting of both body and soul.

Christ told His adversaries, when they had apprehended Him, that they would yet see Him sit on the right hand of power and coming in the clouds of heaven, as John also testifies, "Behold! He comes with the clouds. And every eye shall see Him, and those who pierced Him shall see Him—and all the tribes of the earth shall wail on account of Him" (Revelation 1:7). Now none of these things are yet fulfilled, nor shall they be until His second coming. For though the Jews did see Him when He hung upon the cross, yet He was not then coming in the clouds of heaven, nor did all the kindreds of the earth wail because of Him. No, this is reserved till He comes to judge the world. For then the ungodly shall be so put to it that they would gladly creep into the most invisible rock under heaven, to hide themselves from His face and the majesty of His heavenly presence. Therefore, in order for this to be brought to pass, there shall be a resurrection of the dead, "both of the just and the unjust". Though some men are lulled asleep by their opinion that there shall be no resurrection, yet the Lord will rouse them when He comes. He will cause them to awake, not only out of their false security, but out of their graves, to come to their doom, so that they may receive the reward that is due to their error.

2. The body of the ungodly must arise out of the grave in the last days because that body and their soul were copartners in their lusts and wickedness while they lived in the world. God is a God of knowledge, and actions are weighed by Him. "God shall bring every work into judgment, with every secret thing whether it is good, or whether it is evil"(Eccl. 12:14). And as He will bring into judgment every work, so He shall also bring every worker into judgment, even "the dead, both small and great". It is not in God to lay punishment where there is no fault, nor to punish a part of the damned for the whole. He shall judge the world with righteousness and the people with equity (see Psalm 95:9). "Shall not the Judge of all the earth do right?" (Gen. 18:25). As the body was the partner with the soul in sinning, so shall every one receive the things done in his body, according to what he has done. Therefore He says in another place, "Behold, I come quickly. And My reward is with Me —to give to each according as his work shall be" (Rev. 22:12). There shall therefore be a resurrection of the dead, both of the just and the unjust.

3. The body of the wicked must rise again because the whole man of the unjust is the vessel of wrath and destruction, just as the whole man of the just also is the vessel of mercy and glory. As Paul says, "in a great house there are not only vessels of gold and silver, but wooden and earthen vessels too. And some are to honor, and others to dishonor"(2 Tim. 2:20). Now as he shows us, these vessels to honor are the good men, and the vessels to dishonor are the bad men. For in Romans 9 we see that it is said that God "endured with much long-suffering the vessels of wrath fitted for destruction"(vs. 22). He also further shows us how they are so fitted: "But according to your hardness and stub-

born heart, you are saving up wrath for yourself
in the Day of wrath and revelation of God's righteous Judgment"(Rom. 2:5). And James says that in the last
days, the days of Judgment, this treasure of wickedness shall "eat
their flesh as fire"(5:3). Now then their bodies being the
vessels of wrath, and since they must be so possessed with this
wrath at the last day that their flesh may be eaten with it, it is
evident that their body must rise again out of their grave and appear before the Judgment-seat. For it is from there that each of
them must go, with this full load, to their long and eternal home,
"where their worm dies not, and the fire is never
put out"(Mark 9:44).

4. The severity of God towards His children, with His forbearance toward His enemies while still in this world clearly speaks
of a resurrection of the ungodly—so that they may receive the
just reward for their wickednesses which they have committed
in this world. We read that while "their eyes stand out
with fatness," "the godly are plagued and chast-
ened" all the day long (Psalm 73:7,14). Therefore it is evident that
the place and time of the punishment of the ungodly is in another
world. "If judgment first begins at us, what shall
be the end of those who do not believe the gospel
of God?"(1 Pet. 4:18). If the righteous are scarcely saved, where
shall the ungodly and the sinner appear? Alas! poor creatures! now
they plot against the righteous and gnash upon them with their
teeth, but the Lord laughs at them, for He sees their day is coming, as it is written, "the wicked is kept for the day of
ruin. They shall be brought forth to the day of
wrath"(Job 21:30). Peter says, "The Lord knows how to
deliver the godly out of temptation and to keep
the unjust unto a day of judgment to be punished"
(2 Peter 2:9). And Jude says, "They are wild waves of the
sea foaming out their own shame—wandering stars
to whom the blackness of darkness has been kept
forever"(Jude 13).

The punishment of the ungodly then is reserved until the day of
judgment, which will be the time of their resurrection. Observe,
(A) The wicked must be punished, (B) The time of their punishment
is not now, but at the day of judgment, (C) This day of judgment
must be the same with the resurrection of the dead, at the end of
the world. "So shall it be at the end of the world—
the Son of man shall send forth His angels, and

they shall gather out of His kingdom all things that offend, and those who practice lawlessness. And they shall throw them into a furnace of fire. There shall be wailing and gnashing of teeth" (Matt. 13:43). There shall then be a resurrection of the unjust.

5. The sovereignty of the Lord Jesus over all creatures plainly shows forth a resurrection of the bad, as well as of the good. Indeed the unjust shall not arise because of any relation they have to the Lord Jesus, as the saints shall, but they shall rise because all have been delivered into the hand of Christ and He has been made sovereign Lord over them. Therefore, by an act of His sovereign power, the ungodly must arise. This is Christ's own argument, "the Father judges no one, but has given all judgment to the Son, so that all may honor the Son even as they honor the Father. He that honors not the Son honors not the Father who sent Him" (John 5:22,23). So then they must fall before Him as their sovereign. For He further says, "He gave to Him also authority to execute judgment" (vs. 27). Then He adds, "Do not marvel at this, for the hour is coming in which all those in the graves shall hear His voice and shall come forth—those who practiced good to the resurrection of life—and those who practiced evil to the resurrection of judgment" (vss. 28,29). From this Paul argues, saying, "For to this end Christ both died and rose and lived again, in order that He might rule over both the living and the dead" (Romans 14:9). And "We must all stand before the judgment-seat of Christ" (verse 10).

Mind these words. Jesus Christ by His death and resurrection did not only purchase grace and remission of sins for His elect, with their eternal glory, but He also obtained from the Father to be both Lord and Head over all things, whether they are things in Heaven or things under the earth. He says, "All power in Heaven and earth are given to Me" and, "I have the keys of hell and of death" (Matt. 28:18; Rev. 1:18). So that all things, "whether they are visible or invisible, whether they are thrones or dominions, or principalities or powers; all things were created by Him and FOR Him" (Col. 1:16). This being so, at the name of Jesus every knee must bow and every tongue shall confess that

He is sovereign Lord, to the glory of God the Father. Now, in order that this may be done, He has resolved to have a Judgment Day, in which He will have all His enemies raised out of their graves and brought before Him. In this way He will show His people, His way and His word in their glory. And He will sit in judgment upon His enemies there, and they shall know "who is the blessed and only Potentate, the King of kings, and Lord of lords" (1 Timothy 6:15).

"Behold, the Lord comes with myriads of His holy ones to execute judgment against all, and to convict all the ones who were ungodly among them regarding all their works of ungodliness which they did in an ungodly way—and regarding all the hard things which ungodly sinners spoke against Him" (Jude 15).

6. The great preparation that God has made for the judgment of the wicked clearly demonstrates that they will rise out of their graves, for (1) He has appointed a Day for them to rise; and (2) He has appointed a Judge to judge them; and (3) He has recorded their acts and deads for that Day's testimony; and (4) He has also already appointed the witnesses who are to come in and testify against them; and (5) the instruments of death and misery are already prepared for them.

(1) He has appointed a Day. Soon it will be said, "the time has come for the dead to be judged...to bring to ruin those who have made the earth rotten" (Rev. 11:18). See also Acts 17:31. This time and day is brought down to an hour by Christ, "the hour is coming in which all those in the graves shall hear His voice and shall come forth—those who practiced good to the resurrection of life—and those who practiced evil to the resurrection of judgment" (John 5:28,29).

(2) He has appointed the Judge, "He has set a day in which He is going to judge the world...by the Man whom He ordained" (Acts 17:31). And who is this? It is Jesus Christ, for "it is He who has been appointed by God to be the Judge of living and dead" (Acts 10:42).

(3) He has recorded all their acts and deeds. Not a single ungodly word, not a single idle thought but what is recorded in the books of the laws of Heaven for that day. "The sin of Judah is written with a pen of iron and with the point of a diamond" "Write it in a tablet and note it in a book, so that it may be for the time to come for-

ever and ever that this is a rebellious people" (Isa. 30:8,9).

(4) He has His witnesses for that Day. "For our transgressions are multiplied before You and our sins testify against us," (Isa. 59:12). Shall not those sinned against be there?

(5) He has prepared the instruments of death and eternal misery. "Yes, He has prepared for him the instruments of death; He has made His arrows against the hot pursuers" (Ps. 7:13). Hell has been prepared, He has made it deep and large, and the everlasting fire has been long prepared for it, their judgment is not idling, but is rushing upon them (See Isa. 30:33; 2 Peter 2:3).

But how ridiculous this would all be if the only wise God should have prepared these things and there would be no one to be judged. Sinners would be indeed very glad if things might be this way. They would be glad at heart if they might be in their secret places of darkness and the grave forever. But it must not be. The day of their resurrection is set. The Judge is appointed, their deeds are written, the Lake of Fire waits with open mouth for them. Therefore at the Day appointed neither earth nor death nor Hell can keep them back—"There shall be a resurrection of the dead, both of the just and the unjust" (Acts 24:15).

7. Lastly, I cannot but believe there shall be a resurrection of the wicked at the last day because of the ungodly consequences and errors that most naturally follow the denial of it:

For (1) He who takes away the doctrine of the resurrection of the wicked takes away one of the main arguments that God has provided to convince a sinner of the evil of his ways. For how shall a sinner be convicted of the evil of sin if he is not convinced of the certainty of eternal judgment? And how shall he be convinced of eternal judgment if you persuade him that when he is dead he shall not rise? especially since the resurrection of the dead and eternal judgment must unavoidable be the forerunner of the one before the other. It was Paul's reasoning of righteousness, temperance and judgment to come that made Felix tremble. This was Christ's argument when He says that every idle word that man shall speak shall be judged in the day of judgment (Matt. 12:36).

But it is plain that "there shall be a resurrection of the dead, both of the just and the unjust" (Acts 24:15). And whatever others may say or profess, being beguiled by Satan, and their own hearts, yet make sure that you "fear Him who is able to destroy both soul and body in hell" (Matt. 10:28).

"And the sea gave up the dead in it. And death and Hell gave up the dead in them. And they were judged each according to their works" (Revelation 20:13).

Having shown you that the wicked must arise, now take notice of the manner of their rising. And note that as the very titles of the "just" and the "unjust" are opposite to one another, so are they in all other matters, even in their resurrections.

First, the just come forth in incorruption in their resurrection, but the unjust come forth in their corruptions in their resurrection —The ungodly at their resurrection shall forever after be incapable of having their bodies and their souls separate, nor shall they be annihilated into nothing—yet it shall not be that they may rise in incorruption. For if they arise in incorruption, they must arise to life, and they would also have the conquest over sin and death. But the resurrection of the wicked is called the "resurrection of condemnation" and these shall be "hurt by the second death" —they shall arise in death and shall be under it, under the gnawings and terrors of it. As it were, a living death shall feed upon them. They shall never be spiritually alive, nor shall they be absolutely dead. Just as he who is going before the judge to receive sentence to the gallows is eaten up by the fear of natural death and a soon-coming Hell, because of his guilt, so shall it be forever when he gets there.

In this way the wicked shall come out of their graves, with the chains of eternal death hanging on them, the talons of that dreadful ghost fastened in their souls, so that they shall be as far from spiritual life as Heaven is from Hell. "Their worm never dies and their fire is never quenched" (Mark 9:44). From death to eternity it shall never be put out. Their bed is now in the flames, and when they rise it will be in flames. While they stand before the Judge, it will be in flames, even the flames of a guilty conscience—the ungodly shall be far from rising as the saints —for they are ever in the region and shadow of death, and it is ever feeding on their souls. It is ever presenting to their hearts the heights and the depths of the misery that now must seize them and swallow them up like a bottomless gulf. "They shall come out of their holes like worms of the earth and be afraid of the Lord our God" (Micah 7:17).

2. As the resurrection of the godly shall be a resurrection in glory, so the resurrection of the wicked will be a resurrection of

dishonor. Yea, as the glory of the saints will then be glory unspeakable, so the dishonor of the ungodly at that Day will be dishonor beyond expression. Daniel said that the wicked shall rise "to shame and everlasting contempt"(Dan. 12:2). And again, "O LORD, when You awake You shall despise their image"(Ps. 73:20). Nothing is more loathsome to our eyes than these shall be in the eyes of God.

The ungodly at their death are like the thistle seed, but at their rising they are like the grown thistle—more offensive and provoking than ever. Such dishonor, shame and contempt will appear in them that neither God nor Christ, saints nor angels, will so much as once regard them or attempt to come near them. "He beholds the wicked afar off"—because in the day of grace they would not come to Him and be saved, therefore now they shall all be like thorns thrust away. O how irksome, how dishonorable and contemptible will those be who arise Godless, Christless, without the Spirit and without grace!

3. As the just shall rise in power, so the wicked and unjust shall rise in weakness and faintness and astonishment. Sin and guilt bring weakness in this life, how much more when sin and guilt fasten on them with all their power and force, like a gaint vice. God has said, "Can your hands be strong and can your heart endure in the day that I shall deal with you?" (Ezek. 22:14). The ghastly jaws of despair shall gape upon you then, sinner! The condemning of conscience will continually batter against your weary spirit like thunder-claps! It is the godly that have boldness in the day of judgment. O the fear and the heartache that will seize the wicked when they rise! O the frightful thoughts that will then fill their throbbing hearts! The soul that has been in hellfire must now take again the stinking body and suffering will be even more increased. They shall not be able to lift up their heads forever, "Pangs and sorrows shall take hold of them ....they shall be amazed at one another; — their faces shall be like flames"(Isa. 13:7,8). Everything they see or hear or even think shall bring them pain. They whom God has left must be weak, for guilt and death have seized upon them.

4. As the just shall arise in spiritual bodies, so the unjust shall arise only as lumps of sinful nature—having no help from God to bear them up under this condition. Therefore they will continually feel a sinking under every remembrance of every sin. They shall rise only to fall into that dungeon called bottomless (because there is no end to their misery there). Not separately, but together body and soul are bound in the cords of sin and iniquity, trembling be-

fore God as He sentences them.

THE BOOKS OPENED FOR JUDGMENT

Now when the wicked are raised out of their graves in this way, they shall be brought up together with all the angels of darkness, their fellow-prisoners, being shackled in their sins. There at the place of judgment Jesus Christ, the King of kings and Lord of lords shall sit in judgment upon them, for He is the Lord Chief Judge of things in Heaven and earth, and things under the earth. On His right hand shall sit all the saints and prophets, the apostles and witnesses of Jesus, each one on the throne of glory. Then that which is written shall be fulfilled, "bring here those who were unwilling for Me to rule over them and kill them in front of Me" (Luke 19:27).

When everyone is in his proper place, the Judge on His throne, the saints around Him, the prisoners coming up to judgment, immediately there shall come forth a mighty fire and tempest from before the throne. This fire shall go around the throne as a fence to keep them at a certain distance from the heavenly Majesty. For David wrote, "Our God shall come and shall keep silence; a fire shall devour before Him," (Ps. 50:3). And again, Daniel wrote, "and the Ancient of Days sat, whose robe was white as snow, and the hair of His head like the pure wool. His throne was like the flaming fire, and His wheels like burning fire. A stream of fire went out and came forth from before Him" (Daniel 7:9,10).

This having been done, the Judge upon His throne, His attendants around Him, the bar for the prisoners, and the rebels all standing around with ghastly jaws looking for what was to come, then the books are brought forth. That is, the books of both death and life are brought. And every one of them is opened before the sinners who are now to be judged and condemned. For Daniel continued on, "A thousand thousands served Him and ten thousand times ten thousand stood before Him. The Judgment was set and the books were opened" (v. 10). This scene also appears in Rev. 20:12, "And I saw the dead, small and great, standing before God. And books were opened. And another book was opened, which is the Book of Life. And the dead were judged out of the things written in the books, according to their works".

He does not say that the book was opened, but the books, that is, many books. And indeed the dead shall be judged out of more than one, two, or three books:

1. There is the book of Creation.
2. There is the book of God's Remembrance
3. There is the book of the Law.
4. There is the book of Life.

"And the books were opened" —Revelation 20:12.

1. The book of the Creation shall be opened. And this shall be first, as it concerns man's nature, as it relates to all other creatures.

First, He will show what principles God created in them. Then He will show how contrary to these principles the world walked. The principles of nature are concluded under these three heads:

(1) Man by his own natural reason and judgment may clearly know that there is a God, a deity, a principal being who is over all and supreme above all. Man merely as a rational creature finds this within himself. And so it is that all the heathen nations conclude by natural reason that we are His offspring, that is, that we are His creation and workmanship. Man knows that there is such a God.

(A) by the face that he is able to judge that there is such a thing as sin even in his natural state. Christ said, "why do you not judge what is right even of yourselves?" (Luke 12:57). It is as if He had said, You are degenerated even from the principles of nature and right reason. And Paul writes in another place, "does not even nature itself teach you" (1 Cor. 11:14). Now he that can judge that there is such a thing as sin must of necessity be able also to understand that there is a God, to whom sin is opposite. For if there is no God, there is no sin against Him. And he who does not know the One does not know the other.

(B) by nature man knows there is a God by those fits of fear and dread that are often within themselves. For every man that draws breath in this world is reproved, judged and condemned by his own conscience and thoughts, even though they do not know either Moses or Christ. Paul tells us that the Gentiles (who do not have the Law) still "show the work of the Law written in their hearts, their conscience bearing witness with them" (Rom. 2:15). By this very thing they show that God created them in that state and quality that they might in and by their own nature judge and know that there is a God. And it is written there in Romans 2 that their thoughts, their workings of heart, their convictions of conscience, their accusations, together with the fear that is begotten in them when they transgress the law written in their hearts shall be judged by Jesus Christ (vss. 15 and 16).

Furthermore, the natural proneness of all men to devotion and religion clearly tells us that they themselves read the book of nature and find that there is one great and eternal God.

(2) The second principle of nature is this, that this God should be sought after by men in order that they might enjoy communion with Him forever.

The light of nature shows man that there is a great God, even God who made the world. And the reason that he is shown this is "that they might seek the Lord — if perhaps they might feel after Him and might find Him. Though indeed He is not far from each one of us," etc. (Acts 17:27).

(3) The third principle of nature is this, that men between themselves should do that which is just and equal.

As Moses said long before the Law was given, "why do you strike your fellow?" (Ex. 2:13). As if he should say, "You are of equal creation, you are the same flesh, you both know that it is not just for anyone to do you wrong. Therefore you ought to judge by the same reason that you ought not to wrong others."

Now every man in the whole world has transgressed against every one of these three principles of nature (see Romans 3:10-18).

As to principle number one, who is he that has honored, worshipped, reverenced and adored the living God to the height of what they saw in Him, according to the goodness and mercy they have received from Him? All have instead "worshipped and served the created thing more than the Creator" (Rom. 1:25). They have thus walked contrary to this first principle implanted in them by nature.

As to principle number two, "there is none that seeks after God" (Rom. 3:11), but instead of minding their own future happiness according to the teaching of nature, men have given way to sin and Satan. Natural reason teaches all men to love that which is good and profitable, yet they have loved that which is hurtful and destructive.

As to principle number three, instead of doing to others what he desires to be done unto him, man has given himself up to vile affections. Refusing the dictates of nature, he is "filled with all kinds of unrighteousness — fornication, wickedness, covetousness, malice — being full of envy, murder, quarrels, deceit, evil habits" (Rom. 1:29).

And observe that he does not say that all these things are put into practice by every man. But he says that every man has these in his heart, which there defile the soul and make it abominable in the sight of God. Man, then, having sinned against the natural light and reason, judgment and conscience given him by God, he shall certainly perish (even though he never knew either Moses or Christ). "For as many as sinned without Law shall also be lost without Law" (Romans 2:12).

Yes, here man will be found to be not only a sinner against God, but an opposer of himself, a contradicter of his own nature, — one that will not do that which he judges to be right in his heart. Their sin is written upon the tables of their own hearts and their own backsliding shall both correct and reprove them.

It is marvelous, if we consider how intricate a creature man was made by God, to see how much man acts and does in this state of sin and degeneracy. Man was created in the image of God. But man by yielding to the tempter has made himself the very figure and image of the devil. Man was created upright and sinless. But man by sin has made himself crooked and sinful. Man was created with all the faculties of the soul free to study God his Creator in His glorious attributes and being. But man by sin has imprisoned his own senses and reason and has given way to blindness and ignorance of God that they may reign in his soul. So man is now captured and held in bondage, alienated and estranged from God and from all that is spiritually good. "Because when they knew God they did not glorify Him as God, neither were they thankful. But they became vain in their thoughts and their foolish heart was darkened"(Rom. 1:21). And again, "being darkened in the understanding, being made strangers to the life of God because of the ignorance which is in them, because of the hardness of their hearts" (Ephesians 4:18).

Now man shall be brought forth to the Judgment for this abuse of the workmanship of God. And he shall be convicted, condemned as a rebel against both God and his own soul.

When this part of the book regarding man's nature is opened and man is convicted by it for his sinning against the three general principles of it, then immediately the second part of the book will be opened. This concerns the mystery of the creation. For all of the creation was made not only to show the power of God in themselves, but also to teach us and to preach to us, that we might know more of God and of ourselves. "For God's wrath is revealed from Heaven on all ungodliness and unrighteous-

ness of men, who hold down the truth in unrighteousness. Because that which is known about God
is clearly known within them, for God clearly
showed it to them. For the unseen things of Him
from the creation of the world are clearly seen,
being understood by the things that are made,
both His eternal power and Godhead, in order for
them to be without excuse" (Romans 1:18,19,20).

The various parts of the world, the heavens, the earth, the sun,
the moon, and all the other created things of God, preach aloud to
all men, proclaiming the eternal power and Godhead of their Creat-
or. He has made all of them in wisdom, that they may teach and
instruct men. And he who is wise and desires to understand these
things shall understand the loving-kindness of the Lord. "For the
works of the Lord are great, sought out by all
those who have pleasure in them" (Psalm 111:2).

Secondly, not only does the creation in general preach of God to
every man, but all its parts show men how to behave themselves
before God and one another. Yes, these inanimate things will come
in at the Judgment to witness against all those who have crossed
and perverted the truth which God has taught by His creatures:

(1) They shall witness to you by their obedience to God and to
man.

(A) Except for sinful men and devils, all the creatures are subject to God, even the fiercest animals, the deeps, fire, hail, snow
and vapors, all are fulfilling God's word. And by their obedience
these teach you obedience. Yes, by their obedience your own dis-
obedience shall be condemned at the judgement.

(B) The obedience of the creatures to man teaches you that you
also should be obedient to your superiors. "For every kind
of animals and of birds, both of creeping things
and things of the sea, is tames and has been tam-
ed by mankind" (James 3:7). These obey man, and man only remains untamed, unruly, and therefore is condemned by these.

(2) They shall witness to you by their fruitfulness. All created
things are fruitful, admonishing you to have a fruitful life toward
God. God did but say the word in the beginning, Let the earth bring
forth fruit, etc. and it was so. But He has sent His prophets both
early and late, saying, "do not do this abominable thing
that I hate" (Jer. 44:4), but men will not obey. "Therefore
by their fruits you shall know them" (Matt. 7:20).

(3) The knowledge and wisdom of the creatures shall witness to
you. The stork, the swallow and the crane observe the time and the

season of their coming, thereby admonishing you to learn the time of grace. The ox and the ass both know and acknowledge their master's crib, thereby admonishing you to know and acknowledge the bread and word of God. These shall condemn your ignorance of the food of Heaven.

(4) The labor and toil of the creatures convict you of sloth and idleness. "Go to the ant, sluggard; consider her ways and be wise" (Prov. 6:6). Why? For the ant provides for food in summer and lays up for the day of trial. Yet men spend the whole summer of their existence in wasting the time given for improving their souls. Solomon said, All things are full of labor. Only man spends all the day idle, his years being like a tale that is told. The coney is a feeble animal, yet he labors for a house in the rock. The spider takes hold with her hands and builds an abode in king's palaces. Only man turns himself upon the bed of sloth. It is only man who refuses to take hold of the Rock, even Christ; Man alone will not labor to possess a mansion in the kingdom of Heaven.

(5) The fear of the creature will teach men to flee from the wrath to come. "Surely in vain the net is spread in the sight of any bird" (Prov. 1:17). Yet man lays in wait for his own blood, lurks secretly for his own life. Creatures flee from the natural dangers around them, but man delights to dance around the mouth of Hell. He alone is knowingly and willingly bitten and ensnared by Satan.

(6) The hope of the creatures will witness to you, for they depend upon their God. The ravens look to God for food, as do all creatures, and thus condemn the practices of men. For men imagine that they must lie and cheat, defraud and deceive in order to get those things which God gives to His creatures freely. Men will not hope in God and depend on Him, thus shutting themselves out of God's Heaven.

(7) The tender care of the creatures for their loved ones will condemn the hard-heartedness of men. "The heavens shall reveal his iniquity; and the earth shall rise up against him" (Job 20:27), that is, all the creatures of God will rise up to testify to you that they have been subject to the will of the Creator, showing you what you should have been toward Him.

All these things, as inconsiderable as they may appear to you now, will appear in the Judgment and you shall know that they were given to you as warning=words from God to your souls. This book of the creation is so excellent and so full, so suitable to the capacity of all, that there is not a man in the world but is caught and convicted by it. Though he never saw either New Testament of old,

the most unlearned of men may know much of both God and himself
by reading the creatures. It was out of the book of nature that Job
and his friends discoursed so profoundly of the judgments of God.
It was out of the book of the creation that God preached so con-
vincingly of Himself to Job. This is the book so often used by both
Christ and His apostles to produce similitudes for our conviction
and instruction. Yet, because of the ignorance of men in their sinful state, nothing will work with them but what is set in their heart
by the Holy Spirit.

One more word about the book of the creation. Man himself judges
the creatures in a way that God shall judge man. For if you have a
tree in your garden that does not bear fruit, why do you pass sentence upon it, that it should be cut down? Do you not by this also
pass judgment upon your own fruitless soul? "And even now
the axe is laid to the root of the trees. Therefore every tree not bringing forth good fruit is
cut down and is thrown into the fire" (Matt. 3:10).
For as surely as you say to your fruitless tree, "Cut it down. Why
does it burden the ground?"—so will God say in Heaven, "Cut him
down! Why should he burden the earth?" As men deal with weeds
and rotten wood, so will God deal with sinners in the day of final
judgment. He will bring in all the counsels and warnings He has
given men by the creatures as evidence of His justice and as ag-
gravations of their sinful blindness to His provisions.

THE BOOK OF GOD'S REMEMBRANCE

2. The second book that will be opened at this Day will be the
book of God's remembrance.

For as God has recorded all and every particular good thing that
His people have done toward Him and His name while they were in
this world, so He has also remembered and recorded all the evil
and sin of those who opposed Him. Now God's memory is so perfect
that it is impossible that anything should be forgotten, all shall
be brought forth to the Judgment. As a thousand years are but as
yesterday compared with His eternity, so the sins that have been
committed a thousand years ago are all firmly fixed in the memory
of the eternal God. They are as fresh and clear in His sight as if
they were being committed now. "Hell itself is naked before Him and destruction has no covering" (Job 26:6).
The most secret, the most cunning and hidden plots of the most
subtle of the infernal spirits cannot hide their wickedness from
God's memory. All their ways, their hearts and their most secret
doings, are clear to the very bottom of them in the eyes of the
great God. "All things are naked and opened to the

eyes of Him to whom we must give account"(Heb. 4:13). And He "will bring to light the hidden things of darkness and reveal the thoughts of all hearts (1 Cor.4:5). "they say, The Lord shall not see...Un - derstand, you beastly ones...and you fools, when will you be wise? He who planted the ear, shall He not hear? He who formed the eye, shall He not see?...He who teaches man knowledge, shall He not know? The Lord knows the thoughts of man" (Psalm 94:7-10).

Men remember because they know and see things. This is why God tells us that He will remember all our sins, if we die out of Christ, making it known that He knows and sees all these things, and He will not forget them. So then when the book of God's re- membrance is opened, all things that have been done or thought since the world began shall become manifest. Also all the trans- actions of God and His Son among men shall become known, and this shall be applied to each and every particular person in equity and justice. The sins which you have committed will be your own, and you shall bear them yourself unless you have rolled them upon the Lord Jesus Christ in holy surrender.

All will marvel as the thousands and ten thousands of sins are called forth from their secret places, where you had buried and forgotten them. Yes, God shall show before all those base and horrid deeds which one would not think that any heart would com- mit! Christ said to the Pharisees, "You are they who just- ify themselves before men, but God knows your hearts"(Luke 16:15). Yes, God knows what swarms, what legions of hellish wickedness are now lurking in the breasts of men, yea, even those men that one would swear a thousand times over are good and honest men. The way of men in their sins is as hard to follow as the way of the serpent on the rock or a ship in the midst of the sea, they are so closely hiding and burying under fair pre- tences their filthiness, wiping their mouths and saying "I have done no wickedness".

But God will not be deluded nor blinded nor mocked by all this. He says, "They do not think within their hearts that I remember all their wickedness. Now their own doings have hemmed them in" (Hosea 7:2). Not only the sins of the drunkard, the whoremaster, the thief shall be turned inside outward, but the hearts of every person shall be laid open. Then every sin, with every circumstance of place, time, person, and the causes of every evil shall be revealed to all. The piercing eye of God beholds all places, persons and things. The holy hand of God's justice writes all of them down in the book of His remembrance. And "for all these things God will bring you into judgment" (Ecclesiastes 11:9).

Not only will God bring forth from His book of memory those things which you have done against Him, but He will also bring out those things which He has done for you. You will hear again every sermon which He had preached to you, every chapter that you have read shall come before you. Every conviction that you ever had by the promptings of conscience and every warning that you ever were given in all your life will rise up to haunt you. You will see then the patience of God toward you, how He allowed you to live not one year, two years or ten, but twenty and thirty years to test you. You will remember how many times he rebuked you and chastised you for your wickedness. You will remember how many awakening providences and judgments were laid before your face.

Not only you but all men shall see how many strugglings God had with your heart on your sickbed, and all the vows and promises, all the resolutions you made to God if He would raise you up will again come to your mind. He will show you then how you broke all the chains which He forged to keep you back from fulfilling your lusts. He will open to you how you sinned against light and knowledge, how you labored to put out the light of conscience. O how miserable will the Christless soul be at this Day! All these things will afflict the guilty soul, they will pierce like arrows and bite like serpents.

It makes a man blush to have his pockets searched for stolen goods in the midst of a crowd, especially if he is a reputable man. But here all the heavenly host shall see the shame of every wicked person as God reveals all his hidden sins.

It is one of the greatest mercies of God's covenant of grace that He is willing to forget the iniquity of those who are in Christ Jesus. "Lord, do not remember against us our former iniquities" (Ps. 79:8), is the prayer of all, but only those who rest in Christ will have this heaviest of loads lifted from them. The remembrance of iniquity will be one of the judgments of those who are in Hell.

THE BOOK OF THE LAW

3. The third book that will be opened at this Day is the book of the Law.

This book will especially concern those that have received it, or have had knowledge of it. Not all shall be judged by the book of the

54

Law, but all shall be judged by law. "For as many as have sinned without Law shall also be lost without Law. And as many as have sinned within Law shall be judged by means of Law" (Rom. 2:12). That is, the heathen who never knew the Law delivered at Sinai shall be judged by the law that was written in man's heart in his creation. But those that have knowledge of the law as delivered on Sinai shall be judged by the law as given there.

This book, then, will be terrible in judgment for all those who have known it, far surpassing the two mentioned before. This law is the chief and the most pure resemblance of the justice and holiness of the heavenly Majesty, and it holds forth to all men the sharpness and keenness of His wrath above the other two books. This is because it has been delivered in such plain and open language and covers both the duty commanded and the sin prohibited. Therefore more violence and retribution will fall upon the head of those who have violated or ignored it.

The Law has these two things in it: (1) A discovery of the evil of sin; and (2) A discovery of the vanity of all things which will be used for excuse by sinners at the Judgment.

(1) The apostle tells us that "the Law came in beside in order that the offense might increase" (Rom. 5:20). Thus the offense is discovered to be an offense, as Paul says again, "For I would not have recognized lust unless the Law had said, 'You shall not lust'" (Rom. 7:7). So it is in this life, and so it will be in the day of Judgment. Those that see sin in its abounding nature, in its exceeding sinfulness, must see it by the Law. For this is truly the mirror by which God reveals sin. And those who do not have the happiness to see their sin by the Law in this life, while there is a fountain of grace to wash in and be cleansed, must have the misery to see it at the Judgment. Then nothing is left but the misery and pain and punishment of it. In that Day those little tittles of the holy Law which men now so easily overlook, sinning against them with ease, will each one appear with awesome dread and flaming justice. "It is easier for the sky and the earth to pass away than for one tittle of the law to fail" (Luke 16:17). If such fearful flames and thunderings and storms appeared at the giving of the Law, then what flames and dreadful fears will there be at the execution of the Law! At the giving of the Law all Israel fled, yea, even Moses feared and trembled exceedingly. What, then, will be the feelings of those that God shall judge by His Law in that Day?

O what thunderings and lightnings, what earthquakes and tempests will shake every guilty soul at the opening of this Book! "For behold! The Lord will come with fire and with His chariots like a whirlwind, to refresh His anger with fury and His rebuke with flames of fire" (Isa. 66:15). The Lord will come in the flaming heat of His justice and holiness against sin and sinners, to execute the rigor of His threatenings on their perishing souls.

(2) The second part of this Law is its exactitude—the purity and strictness required of all acts that any poor creature has done in this life, especially those acts of good by which he in the Judgment expects to shelter or secure himself from the wrath of God. This Law is the rule, the plumb line by which every act of every man shall be measured. And he whose righteousness is not found to measure up to this law in every way (which all shall fail to do, for they must have the righteousness of God by faith in Jesus Christ) must perish. As it is written, "Also I will lay judgment to the line and righteousness to the plummet. And the hail shall sweep away the refuge of lies, and the waters shall overflow the hiding place" (Isa. 28:17). That is, though men may now shelter themselves under legal repentance, cold profession, good intentions, imaginations and 'good' deeds, yet all these things must be measured and weighed in the scales against God's most righteous law. And whatever is found not to be "the righteousness of God" will be found to be "a refuge of lies" and will be drowned by the overflowing of the wrath of God. And so at that Day all the ungodly will be found to be as stubble, and the Law shall be as fire: "From His right hand went a fiery law for them" (Deut. 33:2). And again, "Behold, the name of the Lord comes from far, burning with His anger,...His lips are full of fury and His tongue like a devouring fire" (Isa. 30:27). For whatever fire seizes upon, it burns, destroys, devours and consumes. So the Law will seize upon those at that day who will be found to be under the transgression of the least tittle of it.

There are two things which will meet together at the Judgement both in their utmost height and strength: Sin and the Law. For the Judgment shall not come until the iniquity of the world is fully ripe. And when sin has come to its full rottenness, having done all the mischief it can do against the Lord of glory, then God will bring forth His law, His holy and righteous law. One of these is to reign forever. Therefore sin and sinners must tremble, for God will magnify His law and make it honorable; He will give it the vic-

56

are unholy, unjust and bad. So the Lord will by the law rain "s n a r e s
a n d f i r e a n d b r i m s t o n e a n d a h o r r i b l e t e m p e s t on
t h e w i c k e d"(**Ps.** 11:6). This shall be the portion of their cup.

GOD'S MERCY WILL NOT HOLD BACK HIS JUSTICE

Let no one say.then that because God is famous for His mercy—
and patience—He will then fail to be fierce and dreadful in His justice at the day of judgment. Now we see God's goodness and patience
and long-suffering is admirable. But at the Judgment His justice
will be on the stage, and no one knows the power of His anger now.
You may see a few of the sparks of the justice of God against sin
and sinners by noting that He cast off the angels because of sin,
barring them from His presence, condemning them to hell forever .

Now we know that the Law speaks "s o t h a t e v e r y m o u t h
m a y b e s t o p p e d, a n d a l l t h e w o r l d b e u n d e r j u d g-
m e n t t o G o d. F o r t h i s r e a s o n n o f l e s h s h a l l b e
j u s t i f i e d b e f o r e H i m b y w o r k s o f L a w"(Romans 3:19).
O that you might know the Law and the wondrous things that are
written in it! For the Lord will cause that fearful voice to be
heard, "C u r s e d i s e v e r y o n e w h o d o e s n o t c o n t i n u e
i n a l l t h i n g s w h i c h h a v e b e e n w r i t t e n i n t h e b o o k
o f t h e L a w t o d o t h e m"(Gal. 3:10). This curse shall fall on
every one that does not walk in the commandments of God, without iniquity. And none do this except those who walk in Christ, who
alone fulfilled the Law in all its purity.

Yes, the Law stands at the entrance of the paradise of God, as
a flaming sword turning every way to keep out all those who have
not the righteousness of God, those who cannot come to the throne
of grace by that new and living way which Jesus has consecrated
for us through the veil, that is, His flesh (Heb. 10:19). The curse
of this law has been taken away by Christ for all that truly and
savingly believe, but it remains in full force against every soul
that is not clothed in the righteousness of Christ.

So then, only he who can answer all the most perfect and legal
demands of God's law can live in the midst of its devouring power.
Blessed then is he whose righteousness answers to every point of
the law of God, those who are in Christ Jesus, who "w a s m a d e
t o u s w i s d o m f r o m G o d a n d r i g h t e o u s n e s s a n d
s a n c t i f i c a t i o n a n d r e d e m p t i o n"(1 Cor. 1:30). For God
in Himself is a consuming fire (Heb. 12:29), and man, out of Christ,
is but stubble, chaff, thorns, briers, fuel for the wrath of this
holy and sinner-consuming God to seize upon forever. "W h o c a n
s t a n d b e f o r e H i s f u r y? a n d w h o c a n s t a n d u p i n
t h e h e a t o f H i s a n g e r?" (Nahum 1:6).

THE WITNESSES

Now when these three books are opened, there will no doubt be sad throbbing and pricking in every heart that stands before the judgment-seat of Christ, the righteous judge. Without question, they will be studying a thousand ways to evade and shift the stroke, which shall surely fall on them for the sins revealed by the books. But to cut off any excuse, witnesses will immediately appear and give full and soul=killing proof of everything charged against them.

1. The first and chief witness will of course be God Himself. "listen, O earth, and all that is in it. And let the Lord be witness against you, the Lord from His holy temple" (Micah 1:2). He will say, "I have seen all, I know all, and I have written all of it down. There has not been a thought in your heart that I have not known (Ps. 139). All things have been open and naked to My eye. I have watched you and I am well acquainted with all your ways." He will go on to witness against you, "You have not remained in that holy state in which I created you. You have not desired to retain that knowledge and understanding of Me which you had at your creation. You gave way to the lure of evil and your foolish heart was darkened, alienated and estranged from God." He will even say to you, "The other creatures themselves have condemned you, for they have been fruitful when you were fruitless. They have feared Me, but you were foolhardy. They have known their Master, but you have denied Him."

Truly, when God witnesses, "every mouth shall be stopped and all the world shall become guilty before God" (Romans 3:19).

2. But there will be another witness to condemn the transgressor also, even Conscience: "For they shall show the work of the Law written in their hearts, their conscience bearing witness with them" (Romans 2:15). Your conscience will cry Amen to every word that God speaks against you. The witness of conscience is of great authority, fastening guilt on every soul which it accuses. So it is written that conscience condemns us. Even the consciences of the pagan sinners will condemn them. How much more those who have heard the word of God! O the mire and dirt that a guilty conscience can cast up before the judgment-seat of Christ. There will be no peace when God lets loose a man's conscience upon him. He will like Cain cry "My punishment is more than I can bear." For every

charge that God shall charge against you, Conscience will cry out, Guilty! What a damning witness it will be in that Day!

3. A man's thoughts will witness against him in that Day.

(1) His thoughts of God will stand against him. For sometimes he thought that there was no God, like a fool he said in his heart that there was no God (Psalm 14:1).

Sometimes he thought that there was surely a God, but that God was altogether such a one as he was (Psalm 50:21).

Sometimes he thought that God was so impure as to be able to look upon sin, that God would let a man escape punishment for sin in exchange for certain deeds of kindness toward other men; or sometimes he thought that hypocritical tears and howling prayers would deliver him from the fearful hell which he saw gaping and waiting for him.

Sometimes he had right thoughts of God in some partial way, giving Him credit for mercy and love, but hating His justice and holiness. Sometimes he could even see both mercy and justice, but in order to fulfill his own desires, he shut his eyes against truth and hardened his heart against God in order to rush knowingly and willingly into the sin and wickedness his nature yearned to commit.

(2) Not only are his thoughts of God defective, but they are also without steadiness.

Sometimes they think that they are sinners, but again they think that they are righteous enough to stand the judgment of God.

Sometimes they imagine that they shall never die; or, if they do die, then they shall never rise again to stand judgment. Or, if they must rise again, then they shall be somehow saved by something they did or someone else did for them.

Now I say that these thoughts and ten thousand more like them shall be brought in against the Christless sinner in that Day. Then they shall indeed prove to be a lump of confusion, a mass of sin, a budnle of ignorance and atheism, their unbelief laying them open to the severest judgment of God. So God will show them that every imagination and thought of their heart was only evil continually (see Gen. 6:5). He will convict them, He will condemn them because they did not read the Book of Creation, the Book of Remembrance and the Book of Law.

Now then the wicked shall be standing before the judgment-seat on trial for their lives, in view of heaven and hell. And they will then begin to plead for themselves, having heard and seen the witness against them from these other books. And their pleas will be to this effect:

'Lord, we did find in the Scriptures that Thou didst send a Saviour into the world to deliver us from these sins and miseries. And we heard this Saviour preached and openly offered to such poor sinners as we are. Lord, we also made profession of this Saviour and many of us frequented His holy ordinances, eating and drinking in Your presence and teaching in our streets. And, Lord, some of us were preachers ourselves, having prophesied in Your name and even casting out devils in Your name, doing many wonderful works. Yea, Lord, we left the profane and wicked world and kept company among Your people. Lord, Lord! Please open to us!

All the while they are pleading and speaking for themselves in this way, behold! they earnestly groan, looking ghastly as their briny tears flow down from their eyes like rivers. They redouble their petition, Lord! Lord! Lord! Lord!, seeking and striving to "enter in at the narrow gate." But as Christ said, Once the Master of the house has risen up, when He has laid aside His mediation for sinners and has taken upon Himself to judge and to condemn, then the wicked will begin to stand outside and knock, contending for a portion with the blessed ones. O how their hearts will yearn when they look upon the kingdom of glroy! And how painfully they will ache and throb as they look into a gaping hell!

But now to take away all their cavils and objections, the Book of Life is brought out to conclude and give a final end to Judgment. As John wrote, "And another book was opened, which is the Book of Life. And the dead were judged out of the things written in the books, according to their works" (Revelation 20:12).

But this Book of Life is not opened at this time because there are any godly ones to be tried. Their judgment is past and over before the wicked rise. But the Book of Life is opened now for the further conviction of guilty reprobates, in order to stop their mouths forver. For believe it or not they will be again judging, judging God while He is judging them. But He will be justified in His sayings and will overcome. Yet He will not hastily and angrily cast them away, but will conduct a legal and convincing proceeding against them. His truth shall overthrow all their cavils. That is why the Book of Life is opened before them, for it will show them the names of the elect, their conversion, and their truly gospel conduct. This Book will show them that they are not of the number of the elect, that they were never regenerated, and that they never conducted themselves in the world in a way suitable to the gospel. These are the things by which the unsaved must at last be judged:

1. Are you in the Book of Life, where the names of all the elect are recorded? Christ said, "Rejoice that your names are written in Heaven" (Luke 10:20), and again, "in Your book all My members were written" (Psalm 139:16).

Now, then, if your name is not found among the prophets, the apostles, or the rest of the saints, you must be put apart as one that is cast away, polluted and abominable. Your name is lacking in the genealogies and rolls of Heaven. You are not written down for everlasting life, therefore you must be delivered to misery. No soul shall be delivered at this day of God, though they give a thousand worlds, but only those that are found written in this Book of Life. But everyone of those written shall in that Day be delivered from the wrath to come.

O how carefully will the unbeliever now begin to look for his name in this Book. Those that scoffed at all warnings and slighted the counsel of those who asked them to make their calling and election sure will now give all the treasures of the world if they could but find their names among the sons of God written in this Book. But they will fail, they will faint, they will languish in their souls, as they look and see that their names are not there. What pain will race through the heart of Cain as he finds the name of Abel there, but not his own! Absalom will swoon as he sees the name of David there, as well as Solomon his brother. There will be the saddest kind of sadness in the souls of those who find their names are not written in the Book of Life of the Lamb slain from the foundation of the world.

2. Also in this Book will be the record of the nature of conversion; of faith, love, etc. And all those that do not have the effectual work of God upon them, the true and saving operation of grace in their hearts (which is truly the life which is begun in every one of the Christians), will not be found to be written in this Book. Eternal life is already begun in this life in the souls of the saved.

As Christ said, "He that believes in Me has everlasting life," (John 6:47). And again, "He that eats My flesh and drinks My blood has everlasting life—and I will raise him up in the last day" (John 6:54).

So it is that those written in this Book are called "the living."

Here, then, the Lord will reveal what conversion is, in the true and simple nature of it. Then you will see and be convinced that you have missed it. For when you see what a change, what an alteration the work of regeneration makes on every soul and in every heart where the effectual call, the call according to His purpose, comes, then you will know that you have been a stranger to this regeneration and call. Then you cannot but immediately fall down grieving that you have no share in this part of the Book of Life. Only the living are written here. Not one dead, not one carnal, not one of the wicked is recorded in the Book of Life.

No, when the Lord shall mention the Babylonians, the Philistines, and the Ethiopians, then He will say also that you also were born among them. Yes, it shall be said of the ungodly man that he was born there, that he lived and died in the state of nature and so is under the curse of God. For God will at this Day divide the whole world into these two ranks, the children of the world on the one side, and the children of Zion on the other side. "And of Zion it shall be said, This and that man was born in her...the Lord shall count, when He writes up the people, that this man was born there" (Psalm 87:5,6).

But poor will be the soul who for so long judged himself by the crooked rule of his own reason and imagination. O he loved himself and was pure in his own eyes! But now he must be judged only by the words and rule of the Lord Jesus. And at this time these words of Holy Scripture shall not be twisted and perverted, this way and that way, in order to smooth you up in the hypocrite's hope. For whether you are a king or not, whoever you are, the word of Christ shall judge you in the last day, and that with His interpretation.

Sinners will then begin to cry with loud and bitter cries. They will also begin to see the worth of a broken and contrite spirit, the value of walking with God as living ones in this world. But, alas! it is too late for these things to appear in the hearts of the condemned. Christ must indeed be shown to them now, together with the true nature of faith and grace, but it will be when the door is shut and mercy is gone. They will pray and repent most earnestly, but it will be in the time of the floods of eternal wrath.

A CHALLENGE TO SINNERS AND CHRISTIANS

Now tell me, sinner, if Christ should come to judge the world tonight, would you be able to stand the trial of the Book of life? Are you sure that your profession, your conversion, your faith, and all the other graces that you think you have will prove to be true in the day of Judgment? Examine and try yourself, for "He that practices the truth comes to the Light, so that his works may be known, that they have been fashioned in God" (John 3:21).

You say you are a Christian? You say that you have repented, that you believe in and love the Lord Jesus? But will these things be found to be of equal length, height and breadth with the Book of Life when you are weighed? Will you be found lacking? Surely you know how confident the foolish virgins were, yet how they were deceived. They companied with the saints, leaving the gross pollutions of the world, and each one had lamps to shine as they went out to meet the Bridegroom. Yet they missed the kingdom, they were not written among the living in Jerusalem! They did not have the true, powerful, saving work of conversion, of faith and grace in their souls. The foolish take their lamps, but they have no saving grace for oil. So you see how sinners will be tested before the Judgment-seat from these two parts of the Book of Life.

3. Yet another part of the Book is to be opened, the record of those Christian acts which have been done since the time of conversion and turning to Christ. Here will be found the testimony of the saints against sin, their suffering for the sake of God and their love toward other members of Christ. Their patience under the cross, their faithful assembling among the saints, and their encouragements to one another to bear up in the ways of Christ shall be found there (Malachi 3:16).

This is why the Lord told those at Sardis that those among them who stood out to the last gasp, holding out in the faith and love of the gospel, would not be blotted out of the Book of Life. But they would be confessed before His Father, and before His angels, that they had the work of God in their souls.

Now then, when this part of the Book of Life is opened, what can be found in it of the good deeds of wicked men? Nothing! For it is not to be expected that thorns should bring forth grapes, or that thistles should bear figs—so it cannot be imagined that ungodly men should have anything commendable recorded in this part of the Book of Life.

Man, what have you done for God in this world? Are you one who has set yourself against the strong strugglines of pride, lust, covetousness and secret wickedness? And do these strugglings rise from pure love for the Lord Jesus? Or do they come from fear and conviction of sin? Do you struggle against your lusts because you truly love the sweet and holy leadings of the Spirit of Jesus Christ? Are you happy to be led into His blood and death for your justification and deliverance from wrath to come?

What have you denied yourself for the name of the Lord Jesus? What have you lost for the word of God and the testimony of His truth in the world? Were you one of those who sighed and afflicted yourself because of the abomination of the times? Has Christ marked you down as such a one? Are you one of those who cannot be made to forsake the ways of God nor wrong your conscience, even by fear or by flattery? Have you slighted those opportunities offered by Satan and the world because they would have led you to sin, though those sins were wholly secret? These are the men whose praise is in the gospel, whose commendable and worthy acts shall be found recorded in the Book of Life.

Alas! Alas! These things are strange to a carnal and worldly man. Nothing of this sort has been done by him in this life. Therefore, how can any such be recorded in the Book of Life?

So, then, when Christ has opened this Book of Life before them and has convinced the ungodly out of it at that Day, then He will shut it up again, saying, 'I find nothing here that will do you good. You are not of My elect. You are of the sons of perdition.'

The wicked, then, will not find anything to their comfort in the first part of the Book of Life, where the names of the elect are recorded. Nor will they find anything in the second part, where the true nature and operation of effectual conversion, of faith, love and the like are recorded. Neither can anything be found in the third part, in which is recorded the worthy acts and memorable deeds of the saints of the Lord Jesus. For these will be found to be clear and full in the Book of Life, and they will be found to be wrought by God in the hearts of the elect. And their conversion and perseverance shall be opened before the eyes of the wicked, as a witness of the truth of God.

They will see first what a change was found in the souls of the saved, how they clung to God and Christ, to His word and His ways. It shall be seen how purposefully, how unfeignedly, how heartily the child of God opposed, resisted and warred against his dearest lusts and corruptions. In this day the saints are hidden, but in that day they shall be known. It shall be seen how Abraham left his native country to follow the word of God; how Lot stuck to God in the midst of wicked Sodom; how the apostles left all to follow Jesus Christ. It will be seen how the saints patiently took all the afflictions, persecutions and crosses for the kingdom of heaven's sake. It will be revealed how they endured burning, starving, stoning, hanging and a thousand such calamities. It will be clearly shown that they manifested their love to their Lord and His cause and His people in the worst of times, in those days when they were most rejected, slighted and abused. The King will say to these, in front of the devil and all condemned sinners, "Come, the blessed of My Father, inherit the kingdom prepared for you from the foundation of the world. For I was hungry, and you gave Me to eat. I was thirsty and you gave Me to drink. I was a stranger, and you took Me in. I was naked, and you clothed Me. I was sick, and you visited Me. I was in prison, and you came to Me" (Matt. 25:34,35). Yes, they owned Christ, stood by Him, denied themselves, nourished all His children, however lowly and weak and despised they may have been. And the world shall see this witness against themselves and will be forced to confess that they are both Christless and graceless. For they will be found to be strangers both in the Book of Life and in the work of the Spirit in the hearts of those holy souls.

Even in this world, these saints of Christ are testifying to the world of their conversion, by the fruits of regeneration. And in doing so they show the unconverted that they are Christ-filled, having salvation. But, alas! They evade this testimony, denying both our happiness and their misery, calling faith only a figment of our imagination, saying that communion with God is only a delusion. Yea, our sincere profession of God's word before the world is but hypocrisy, pride and arrogancy in their sight. But when they see us on the right hand of Christ, sitting with the angels of light— when they see themselves on His left hand, sitting with the angels of darkness—then they will see that our hearts and our ways were clearly opened before their eyes in this life. Yes, the Judge shall show that our hearts were honest and our ways were good, those ways which they hated, slighted, disowned and condemned. What can they say? They will say that they were fools, madmen to miss the way so plainly laid out before them.

And truly was it not for this that the new creation was so plainly revealed, the working of God at the conversion of ungodly men that others might be convinced of the evil of their ways—or, that they might be left without excuse in the day of judgment. God, by lengthening out the life of His people scattered here and there, is making work for the day of judgment, for He will by the conversion, life, patience, self-denial and heavenly-mindedness of His dear children give the wicked a heavy and most dreadful blow. For by this laying bare the work of grace in the Christian's heart, and plainly revealing in His word the mind of Christ, there will be left no ground for pleading that such and such gifts and abilities are due a reward. At that Day they will see that gifts and grace are two wholly different things. For the graceless shall perish, however excellent may have been their gifts. A man may be used as a servant in the church of God and may receive many gifts and much knowledge of the things of Heaven, and still, at last, he may be no more than a bubble, a nothing.

Yes, at that Day they shall clearly see the difference between the excellencies of men and the excellencies of God. Our day does indeed abound with men who are gifted. There are many sparkling wits to be seen today, in every corner. The word of Christ is at their finger's end, but alas! They have nothing but wits and gifts. What religion they have is in their tongues and heads.

THE CONDEMNED DO NOT OBJECT TO ELECTION

Among all the objections and cavils to be made by the ungodly in

66

that Day of the Lord Jesus Christ, there will not be one word said about election and reprobation. They will not murmur at all that they were not predestinated to eternal life. And the reason is this, that they will see then that God could have without prejudice toward the condemned chosen or refused at His good pleasure. Besides, there they will be convinced that there was so much reality and downright willingness in God in every tender of grace and mercy to the worst of men (so much goodness, justness and reasonableness in every command of the gospel of Christ so often preached to them in a tender entreaty for them to embrace it), that they will then be drowned in the conviction that they refused love, grace and reason. They refused love for hatred; loved sin instead of grace; desired unreasonable and worthless things instead of that which was reasonable in the sight of God. Now they shall see that they left glory for shame; left God for the devil; left Heaven for hell; sought darkness instead of light.

Yes, they shall see that they made themselves beasts, though God made them upright and reasonable creatures. God could reasonably have expected them to delight in the things that are good according to God. Now they shall see in spite of the fact that God drew them toward Heaven against their hearts and wills, they loved their sins more than God, and God was not guilty of infusing anything into their souls that in the least hindered, weakened or obstructed them from seeking the welfare of their souls. In this life men may indeed prattle at a mad rate, saying that election and reprobation cause all those not elected to be damned, that God is to blame. But at that Day, they will see that they are condemned because they sinned, not because they were not elected. They will see that God did not put any weakness into their souls, but that He made them pure and holy and just, and that they wilfully, knowingly and desperately listened to Satan and his suggestions, turning away from the holy word of God so carefully delivered to them.

Yes, sinner, you will see that God has at times fastened His cords around your heads and your heels and your hands, by godly education, by smarting convictions, yet you rushed away from all with violence, saying, "Let us break their bands in two, and cast away their cords from us" (Psalm 2:3). God will be justified in His sayings and will be clear when He judges, though now your proud ignorance thinks it can multiply frivolous objections to His condemnation of your soul.

THE LABORS OF THE GODLY WILL CONVICT
The nature of the conversion of the godly in their hearts will

be a witness of the non-conversion of the wicked. But to increase their conviction, there will also be opened before them all the labors of the godly, both ministers and others, with the pains they have taken to save, if it had been possible, these poor wretches. Then it will come like hot burning coals upon their souls that they have often been forewarned of this Day. Never was any judgment proclaimed more publicly than this One. Every sermon that you have ever heard, every discussion of the things of eternity, all will be charged before you as this Judgment begins. Every exhortation of every minister you ever heard, which you have cast away as you heard it, will be witnessed against you. God will multiply His witnesses against you.

YOUR OWN WORDS WILL WITNESS AGAINST YOU

1. Your own vows and promises will witness against you, that you destroyed your own soul, contrary to the light and knowledge that you had. As Joshua said to the children of Israel when they had said that Jehovah should be their God, "You are witnesses against yourselves that you have chosen Jehovah, to serve Him. And they said, We are witnesses" (Joshua 24:22). You shall remember what you have said and promised in regards to God in that Day.

2. Each time you have spoken well of godliness, and yet have gone on in wickedness, shall be found to witness against you. Each time you have condemned sin in others, yet not refraining from sin yourself, you shall find it will witness against you. Every word and every thought of God will witness against you in that Day of Jesus Christ. As Christ said, "But I say to you that every idle word that men shall speak, they shall give an account of it in the day of judgment. For by your words you shall be justified, and by your words you shall be condemned" (Matthew 12:36,37).

Most all will say that serving God and loving Christ and walking in the ways of holiness are best, that best will come of them. Even men who are grossly wicked themselves will yet condemn drunkenness, lying, covetousness, pride and whoring in others. Yet, they continue to be neglecters of God and embracers of sin themselves. Such souls pass judgment upon themselves each time they speak well of godliness, continuing in their sins. As they pass judgment on the sins of others, they also pass judgment on themselves. As it is written, "I will judge you out of your own mouth, wicked servant" (Luke 19:22). You knew what I was, that I de-

68

mand that all be zealous and active for Me, that at My coming I might have received again what I gave you and more. You should have been busy in My work, for My glory and your own good. But since you have against your own light, contrary to what you said with your own mouth, sought your own glory, worked for your own self, then let the holy angels take you, you unprofitable servant, and throw you out into utter darkness—where there shall be weeping and the gnashing of teeth forevermore. He sinned against My will, now he shall go to hell against his will.' So will say the Lord at that day —"He that knows to do good and does not do it, to him it is sin" (James 5:17).

Many more witnesses might be counted up but these will at this time be enough, "At the mouth of two witnesses or three witnesses shall he that is worthy of death be put to death" (Deuteronomy 17:6).

So then, when the books have been opened, the laws have been read, the witnesses have been heard, and the ungodly have been convicted, the Lord and Judge, even Jesus Christ, will proceed to the execution. To that end, He shall pass the sentence of eternal death upon them, saying, "Go away from Me, you cursed, into the everlasting fire which has been prepared for the devil and his angels" (Matt. 25:41). 'You are now,' He shall say, 'adjudged guilty by the Book of Creation, by the Book of God's Remembrance, by the Book of Life. You are guilty of treason against God and Me, murderers of your own souls, as these faithful witnesses have testified. You never had a saving work of conversion upon you, had no faith in Me, and you died in your sins. I have made a thorough search among the records of the living and I find nothing of you, or of your deeds, in them. Go away from Me, cursed ones.'

So at last these poor ungodly creatures will be stripped of all hope and comfort, and they must fall into great sadness and wailing before the Judge. As a drowning man will catch hold of anything, though it may tend to hold him under water and drown him faster, so these poor creatures will whine with one more faint and weak groan, saying, "Lord, when did we see You hungry, or thirsty, or a stranger, or naked or sick, or in prison, and did not then serve You?" (Matt. 25:44).

You see, then, how the sinner will hate to let go of everlasting life. He who once could not be persuaded to close with the Lord Jesus, though one should have persuaded him with tears of blood, now will cling fast to the Lord with arguments and mournful groans to gain time and defer his execution. "Lord, Lord, open to us. He will say, I do not know you. Where are you from? Then you will begin to say, We ate and we drank before You. You have taught in our streets. And He will say, I tell you, I do not know where you are from—depart from Me, all you workers of unrighteousness." (Luke 13:25-27).

Depart! O this word, Depart! How dreadful it is! With what sad weight it will fall on the head of every condemned sinner. For you must note that while the ungodly stand before the Judge, they cannot but have a clear view of both the kingdom of Heaven and of the condemned in hell. At once they shall see the God of glory, the King of glory, the saints of glory, the angels of glory, and the glorious kingdom where all these shall live in joy forever. They will begin to see the worth of Christ, what it means to be separated from Him. They shall also see the pit, the bottomless Lake of Fire, the brimstone and the flaming beds that Justice has prepared for them. They will see their companions in evil, they will know now who are the devils and who are the damned.

Depart then looks two ways, 'Depart from Heaven,' means, 'Depart to hell.' To depart from life means to depart to death. All authority in Heaven and earth has been given to the Saviour, and He now turns them into hell with a "Depart from Me," for they are cursed ones indeed. He would have done them good once, but they despised the good He would do. Now they desire Him to do them good, but He will not. They are forsaken now, God has left them, they are vessels of wrath for being despisers of God and His goodness. Now they lie open to the stroke of justice for their sins. Vengeance now must feed on them, for in the world they fed on sin, treasuring up wrath against this day of wrath, this day of revelation of the righteous judgment of God.

"Depart, you cursed, into everlasting fire" (Matt. 25:41). Fire is that which of all things is most insufferable and insupportable. That is why fire is used to describe the grievous state of the ungodly after Judgment. Who can abide fire? Yet this the wicked must do. Again, not only fire, but everlasting fire. Behold! How great a fire a little sin, a little pleasure, a little unjust dealing has kindled! That is why the fire into which the condemned fall is called the Lake of Fire. Little did the sinner seriously think that when he was sinning against God he was making provision like this for his soul. Now it is too late to repent—His worm must never die, his fire shall never be quenched. The time to commit sin is short, but the time to punish sin is long, even everlastingly long.

"into everlasting fire, prepared for the devil and his angels," in this fire prepared for the devil and his angels, there is a further conviction upon the consciences of the condemned. It is as if God is saying, 'The devil in his creation is far more noble than you, yet when he sinned I did not spare him. I cast him down from Heaven to hell and hung the chains of everlasting darkness upon him. From this, you should have known to take heed, but you would not. Therefore, since you have sinned as he sinned, you are bound over to the eternal punishment, the same justice that you heard was given to him.' The prince of this world has been judged, therefore the world should be convinced of judgment. If they do not heed it now, then they shall hear the eternal sentence rattle in their ears and feel the smart of it.

God shows men what mercy is and what justice is, showing both to others in the plain sight of all. If they are stupid and careless in the day of forbearance, they must learn at last in the day of rebuke and vengeance. God gave the old world 120 years warning by the preparation of Noah. But they were careless, they would not heed the warning of God, therefore He brought in the flood upon the world of the ungodly. In the last day, such a judgment shall be brought upon all workers of iniquity, all shall be swept away in their willful ignorance.

God has prepared this fire for the devil and his angels, they cannot escape it. Hell-fire is no new thing. You cannot plead that you never heard of it. Depart from it by coming to Me, or at that Day I shall say to you, Depart from Me and go into hell-fire.

THE FINAL JUDGMENT

All must now go to their eternal stations. This great company of unbelievers must now fall into their proper place, into the hell of hell. And they drop into it like a stone into a well, for all hope being now taken from them, they must fall with violence into the jaws of eternal desperation, which will deal far worse with a soul, even making much greater slaughter in tortured consciences than the lions could possibly do with the men cast to them.

This is what Paul calls "e t e r n a l j u d g m e n t," because it is last and final. God executes many judgments among the sons of men, many of these continuing for a while but none are eternal. The very devils in hell, though theirs is the longest and most terrible of all the judgments of God yet, must still pass under another judgment on the final judgment day. Some judgments proved beneficial to those judged, being instruments of conversion to some. But as in the severer judgments of men, when there is one final judgment, such as beheading a man, so in the judgments of God, there is one last Judgment. This shall be when the wicked hear that last word, D e p a r t f r o m M e. This word and the voice of the Lord will stick longest and with most power on their slaughtered souls. There will be no calling of it back again. It is the very wind up of eternal judgment.

So, then, when the judgment is over, the mediatorial kingdom will cease to be in the hand of the man Christ Jesus. For as judges here on earth complete their term of duty and then turn in their commissions, so Christ the Judge now delivers up His kingdom to His Father. And now all is swallowed up in eternity. The condemned are swallowed up in eternal justice and wrath. The saved are swallowed up in eternal life and felicity. And the Son delivers up the kingdom to the Father, and as man He Himself is subject under the Father, who had put all things under Jesus. And now God may be all in all.

For now the end has come, even the end of the reign of death. For death and hell and sinners and devils must now go together into the Lake that burns with fire and brimstone. And this is the end of Christ's reign as the Son of man, and the end of the reign of the saints with Him in His kingdom; the kingdom which He has received from the Father for His work, the work which He did for the Father and for the elect: "then comes the end—whenever He delivers up the kingdom to Him who is God and Father—whenever He shall have put down all rule and all authority and power. For it behoves Him to reign until He shall have put all enemies under His feet. The last enemy put down is death" (1 Cor. 15:24-26). This will not be until the final sentence and judgment are over. "For God has put all things in subjection under His feet. But when it is said that all things are put in subjection, it is plain that it excepts Him who put all things in subjection to Him. And when all things shall have been put in subjection to Him, then the Son Himself will be subject to Him who put all things under Him—so that God may be all in all" (1 Cor. 15:27-28).

Now when things come to this, namely, when everyone is in his proper place: God in His place; Christ in His; the saint in his; the sinner in his; let me conclude with a brief touch on both the state of the good and the bad after this eternal judgment.

1. The righteous will never ever fear anything again, not death, nor devil, nor hell. The wicked shall never ever hope again, not for life, nor for happiness or ease of any kind.

2. The holy shall be in everlasting light, but the sinner in everlasting darkness. He shall be without light, yet in fire; ever burning, yet never consumed; always afraid, vehemently desiring to be

annihilated into nothing. He shall ever desire the ease and comfort of the saint, yet he cannot stand to think of it, because he has lost it forever. He shall be loaded with the delight of sin, yet it is his greatest torture. He will always be trying to put sin out of his mind, yet he knows he must ever abide under it, its guilt and its torment.

3. The saints will forever be inflamed with the grace of God which they embraced (as His gift); the wicked shall be flamingly tormented ty thoughts of having rejected and refused His grace.

4. The just will be comforted when they think of their sins, having been delivered from them and forgiven for them. But the wicked will never be comforted, gnawing upon themselves when they think of deliverance and forgiveness in Christ Jesus.

5. When the godly think of hell, it will increase their comfort. But when the wicked think of Heaven, it will sting them like a scorpion. O what wouldn't the damned soul give, though after a thousand thousand years, to put an end to this eternal judgment! But they have an unending misery because they have sinned against a God that is eternal. They have offended that justice that will never be satisfied now, and therefore they must remain in the fire that never shall be put out. Here is judgment, just and sad.

DEGREES OF JUDGMENT

Again, as it will be so with good and bad in general, so it shall be in particular. When the wicked are judged and condemned and have been received into the fiery gulf, then they will find that he who busied himself to sin shall have more wrath and torment than those less guilty. For as doing good abundantly enlarges the heart to receive and to hold more of God's glory, so the doing of evil in abundance also enlarges the heart and soul of the evildoer to receive and to hold more of God's punishment. That is why you read such warnings in the Scriptures as these:

"I say to you that it shall be more bearable for the land of Sodom in the day of Judgment than for you" (Matt. 11:24)—that is, than for those that had sinned against much greater light and mercy, for these "shall receive a greater judgment" (Matthew 11:14).

Does it not stand to reason that he who has most light, most conviction, most means of conversion, who is highest towards Heaven, will have the greatest fall and so sink deepest into the jaws of eternal misery? As one saint differs from another in Heaven, so one damned soul shall differ from another in hell. Even among the devils themselves, there are some worse than others. Beelzebub is the chief of the devils; that is, the one that was most glorious in Heaven, chief among the reprobate angels before his fall—therefore he sinned against the greater light, mercy and goodness. So he became the chief for wickedness and will have as his wages the most terrible of God's torments. That which was said about Babylon shall be true of the condemned in hell:

"As much as she glorified herself and lived in luxury, so much torment and sadness give to her" (Rev. 18:7). Can it be imagined that Judas should not have more torment, having betrayed the Prince of life, the Saviour of the world? Others never came near his wickedness by ten thousand degrees. Again it is written, "that servant who knew the will of his Master, and did not make ready, nor did according to His will, shall be beaten with many stripes" (Luke 12:47); his stripes shall be more than others who through ignorance committed sins worthy of stripes.

But why should I talk of the degrees of the torments of the condemned souls in hell? For he who suffers least will have the waters of a full cup wrung out to him. The least measure of wrath will be the wrath of God. It will be the eternal and fiery wrath, the insupportable wrath of a holy God. It will lay the soul in the gulf of that second death, which will forever have the mastery over the poor sinking, perishing sinner.

"And death and hell were cast into the Lake of Fire. This is the second death. And if anyone was not found written in the Book of Life, he was thrown into the Lake of Fire" (Revelation 20:14,15)

www.ingramcontent.com/pod-product-compliance
Lightning Source LLC
Chambersburg PA
CBHW031608040426
42452CB00006B/445